FAMILY BUSINESS
by Julian Mitchell

CW00362413

First performed at Watford Palace
from 7 – 22 October 2011 and (
from 25 – 29 October 2011

Cast (in order of appearance)

William	Gerard Murphy
Solomon	Ben Onwukwe
Tom	Chris Kelham
Jane	Tessa Churchard
Kate	Anna O'Grady
Hugo	Tom Berish

Director	Matthew Lloyd
Designer	Ruari Murchison
Lighting Designer	Jason Taylor
Sound Designer	Steve Mayo
Deputy Stage Manager	Maddie Baylis
Assistant Stage Manager	Ian Grigson

Scenes

A converted barn on the Welsh Borders

Act 1 – Afternoon
Act 2 – Later that day

With thanks to Waterstones Watford, Sam Kordbacheh
and Natasha Peyton-Bruhl

Family Business

Julian Mitchell introduces his new play:

Part of me feels I have to see the whole world, to explore every variety of culture, of animal and bird, art and architecture, before I can decide how to live in it properly. So I always travel hopefully, as though the secret of life may lie around the next corner, across the next river, over the next range of hills. But another part tells me that this is absurd. 'I am a traveller, you are a tourist, he is a tripper' goes the saying, and a tourist is the most I have ever been. As an outsider, an observer, I have never got to understand more than the superficialities of the societies I've dipped into. And tourism today, with its all too casual wasting of the earth's resources, is becoming morally disreputable. I ought to give up all flying, stay at home, and ride a bicycle instead of polluting the atmosphere with an inefficient car – which would be better for me anyway.

I can't help noticing, though, that most of the world ignores the evidence of climate change, and continues carelessly on its way towards potential self-destruction. Our political leaders are too afraid of losing their seats to confront the public with the issues; our bankers and businessmen never look beyond their immediate profits; and there is very little opportunity or encouragement for us as individuals to take any action. So I am torn between self-indulgence and responsibility, between greed and green. It is this conflict which gave me the idea of writing a play about a family in the travel business, and a play meant embarking on a different form of travel – internal rather than external – exploring individual characters rather than countries, and how we think and feel about sex and marriage and parenting, the basics of family life.

Attitudes have changed so rapidly in the last century that the British society to which Sigmund Freud came as a refugee in 1938 now seems as formalised and hidebound as ancient Egypt. If he came back today he would surely be astounded by how much we take for granted of his and his followers' insights about human behaviour. Things which in his day were secret and shameful are now openly discussed. He might even be shocked at the freedom with which we deal with them. Yet human nature hasn't changed. Inner and outer exploration – those are the subjects of Family Business.

Julian Mitchell, July 2011

Cast Biographies

Gerard Murphy William

Gerard Murphy has worked extensively in the theatre as an actor. He is an Associate Artist of the Royal Shakespeare Company where his roles included Oedipus, Petruchio, Dr Faustus, Oberon and Prince Hal.

He has acted in all the major theatre companies in Britain and played Salieri in Amadeus, Lear in King Lear, George in Who's Afraid of Virginia Woolf, Falstaff in Henry IV Parts I and II, Jack in The Weir and Pozzo in Waiting for Godot. Most recently Gerard played Hector in a tour of Alan Bennett's The History Boys, directed by Christopher Luscombe and Sir Lucius O'Trigger in The Rivals, directed by Sir Peter Hall at Theatre Royal Haymarket.

His television work includes Spooks, Trial and Retribution, Waking the Dead, Vanity Fair, McCallum, Father Ted and The Scarlet Pimpernel. Among his films are Batman Begins, Pumpgirl and the Hollywood blockbuster Waterworld.

Gerard's extensive recordings include narrating the BBC's Lord of the Rings, two series of Dickens Confidential and the comedy series Ballylennon.

Gerard has directed plays in Japan, America and Scotland, as well as in England, and he enjoys translating French plays into English.

Ben Onwukwe Solomon

Ben's theatre credits include The Making of Moo (Orange Tree Theatre), High Life (Hampstead Theatre), In Time (Eastern Angles/Tiata Fahzodi), Waking Waterfall (Tiata Fahzodi), Days of Significance (RSC), The Winter's Tale, Pericles (RSC), Macbeth (Out of Joint), The Best Man (Arts Depot), Doctor of Honour (Cheek by Jowl), Play Without Repeats (Orange Tree Theatre), Greenland (National) and The Emperor (Royal Court).

His television work includes Law & Order UK, Coronation Street, Holby City, Doctors, After You've Gone, The Bill, London's Burning and Between The Lines, and his film work includes Late Bloomers.

His radio work for the BBC includes numerous classic series. He is a regular in Radio 4's The Ladies' No1 Detective Agency.

Chris Kelham Tom

Chris trained at The Guildford School of Acting and was a recipient of the Carleton Hobbs BBC Radio Drama Award. Since then he has appeared in numerous radio plays for the BBC, including six series as Howard in Ladies of Letters for BBC Radio 4, Toby in Amy's View (original West End cast), Romeo in Romeo and Juliet (National Audio Drama Award), Wuthering Heights and several Woman's Hour readings. Audio Books include Shatter, David Mitchell's No.9 Dream and Ghostwritten.

His theatre credits include Time of My Life (Watford Palace Theatre), Brecht – Poetry and Song (King's Place, London), Another Country (Arts Theatre), Paresis (Bristol Old Vic), Scenes From An Execution (Hackney Empire), Ignatius Trail (Lyric Hammersmith/Royal Exchange, Manchester), The Dresser (Watford Palace Theatre), A Christmas Carol (National reading tour).

His television credits include Hustle, Trial and Retribution, Last Voices Of A Generation for the BBC. Film includes The Cost Of Love, Over The Edge, What's your Name 41. Chris has also appeared in numerous readings with Actors For Human Rights.

Tessa Churchard Jane

Tessa's theatre credits include The 39 Steps (Criterion Theatre), Brighton Beach Memoirs and Blithe Spirit (Watford Palace Theatre), The Fabulist (Old Red Lion), Lady of Leisure (Liverpool Playhouse), As You Desire Me (Playhouse Theatre), Galileo's Daughter, Man and Superman, Don Juan (Peter Hall Company, Bath Theatre Royal), Still Life/The Astonished Heart (Liverpool Playhouse), Noises Off (Piccadilly and Comedy Theatres), Remember This (National Theatre), Communicating Doors, Lady Windermere's Fan (Theatre Royal, Northampton), Point Of Death (Liverpool Playhouse), The Diary of Anne Frank (Basingstoke Haymarket).

Her film and television credits include Call the Midwife (BBC), Doctors (BBC), The Grain Chest (CK Productions), Family Affairs (Talkback Thames), Casualty (BBC), Mummy (NFTS), Harringham Harker (BBC), Jeeves and Wooster (ITV) and The Bill (Talkback Thames).

Anna O'Grady Kate

Anna graduated from LAMDA in the summer of 2009.
Anna's theatre credits include Stephanie in Time of My
Life (Watford Palace Theatre), Birthday Letters (RSC –
Workshop). Her film and television credits include Black
Pond and Holby City.

Tom Berish Hugo

Tom graduated from LAMDA in 2010. Professional theatre
credits include Romeo and Juliet (Royal Lyceum), Lines
(Rosemary Branch) and After the End (BAC). Credits while
training include Sexual Perversity in Chicago, An Inspector
Calls, The Thousand and Second Night and The Glory of
Living.

Creative Team Biographies

Julian Mitchell Writer

Family Business is Julian Mitchell's tenth produced stage play. Among the other nine are Half-Life, which starred John Gielgud, and Another Country, with Rupert Everett and Kenneth Branagh, which won the SWET award for best play of 1981. Daniel Day-Lewis and Colin Firth later took over main roles, and Everett and Firth starred in the film. In 1986 he wrote After Aida for the Welsh National Opera, which starred Richard Griffiths, Zoë Wanamaker and Ian Charleson. August, his version of Chekhov's Uncle Vanya, directed by and starring Anthony Hopkins, was performed in 1994. His adaptation of Ford Madox Ford's The Good Soldier had its world premiere at Bath Theatre Royal in 2010. His films include his own adaptations of Another Country and August, Arabesque, Vincent and Theo and Wilde.

He has published six novels, the last of which, The Undiscovered Country, was reissued last year.

Among his many original television plays are Shadow in the Sun (Emmy 1971) in the series Elizabeth R (with Glenda Jackson), A Question of Degree, Rust, the series Jennie, Lady Randolph Churchill (with Lee Remick), Abide With Me (with Catherine Nesbitt; International Critics Prize, Monte Carlo and US Humanities Award, 1977), and Survival of the Fittest. He has also adapted many books, including The Weather in the Streets, Staying On (with Trevor Howard and Celia Johnson), and The Good Soldier. He wrote ten episodes of Inspector Morse and the widely acclaimed Consenting Adults starring Charles Dance and Samantha Bond, for which he won the Best Writing Award at the Scottish BAFTA Awards 2007.

He has lived in Monmouthshire for 30 years, where he is a local historian. He curated and wrote the catalogue of the exhibition The Wye Tour and Its Artists, at Chepstow in 2010.

Matthew Lloyd Director

After graduating from Oxford University, Matthew went on to pursue Graduate Studies at Harvard and Columbia Universities. Since 2002 Matthew has been the Artistic Director of the Actors Centre. He was formerly Artistic Director of the Royal Exchange Theatre, Manchester (1997 – 2001), during which period the Exchange won the Barclays TMA Award for Theatre of the Year, and where his credits included All's Well That Ends Well, Waiting for Godot, The Illusion and the award-winning An Experiment with an Air-Pump. He was previously an Associate Director of the Hampstead Theatre (1991 – 1997), where his work included the multi-award-winning The Fastest Clock in the Universe. Productions include The Good Soldier (Theatre Royal Bath); The Line (Arcola Theatre); Duet for One (Almeida Theatre/Vaudeville Theatre); The Flint Street Nativity (Liverpool Playhouse); Hedda Gabler (West Yorkshire Playhouse/Liverpool Playhouse); Copenhagen, Blithe Spirit (Watford Palace Theatre); A Doll's House (West Yorkshire Playhouse); The Lucky Ones (Hampstead Theatre – Olivier and Critics' Circle Award) and The Eleventh Commandment (Hampstead Theatre).

Ruari Murchison Designer

Ruari has designed productions in Helsinki (Finland), Washington DC, the Stratford Festival (Canada), Stuttgart (Germany), Luzern (Switzerland), Haarlem (Holland), Elsinore (Denmark) and many regional theatres in the United Kingdom. Recent design credits include Bette and Joan (Arts Theatre); Romeo and Juliet, Love on the Dole (Octagon Theatre), Mappa Mundi (National Theatre); Titus Andronicus (Royal Shakespeare Company); Othello (Trafalgar Studios); The Solid Gold Cadillac (Garrick); A Busy Day (Lyric Theatre); Peggy Sue Got Married (Shaftesbury Theatre); The Snowman (Peacock Theatre); Toyer (Arts); The Three Sisters on Hope Street, The Glass Room, Gone to LA (Hampstead Theatre); Pravda, The Critic, The Real Inspector Hound (Chichester); The Good Soldier, Master Class (Theatre Royal Bath Productions tour); Deep Blue Sea (West Yorkshire Playhouse); An Enemy of the People (Theatr Clwyd); Arthur and George, Cling to Me Like Ivy, Uncle Vanya, A Doll's House, the David Hare trilogy – Racing Demon, Absence of War, Murmuring Judges (TMA Best Design nomination 2003), The Tempest, Macbeth, Hamlet, His Dark Materials, Arthur and George (Birmingham Repertory Theatre); Intemperance, Tartuffe (Everyman and Playhouse Theatres, Liverpool); Time Of My Life, Mrs Reynolds and the Ruffian, Copenhagen, Alfie (Watford Palace Theatre). His opera credits include Der Freischütz (Finnish National Opera); Peter Grimes, Così fan tutte (Luzerner Opera); La Cenerentola, Il Barbiere di Siviglia (Garsington); L'Italiana in Algeri (Buxton); Les Pèlerins de la Mecque, Zazà (Wexford). His ballet credits include: Bruise Blood (Shobana Jeyasingh Dance Company); Landschaft und Erinnerung (Stuttgart Ballet, Germany); The Protecting Veil (Birmingham Royal Ballet); The Snowman (Seoul, London, Birmingham Rep, touring).

Jason Taylor Lighting Designer

Jason's theatre credits includes; Journey's End (West End/Tour/Broadway); Top Girls (Chichester Festival Theatre); The Invisible Man (Menier Chocolate Factory); The Empire (Royal Court); Six Degrees of Separation, National Anthems (Old Vic); The Merry Wives of Windsor (Globe USA/UK tour); The Big Fellah (Out of Joint); Rum and Coca Cola (West Yorkshire Playhouse/ English Touring Theatre tour); Flashdance (Tour); The God of Hell (Donmar); Burn/Chatroom/Citizenship (National); Pygmalion (Broadway); Jeffrey

Bernard is Unwell, The Good Soldier, Entertaining Angels, Single Spies, Balmoral, The Lady in the Van, Abigail's Party, How the Other Half Loves, Victory (Theatre Royal Bath); Noises Off, Year of The Rat, Little Shop of Horrors (West Yorkshire Playhouse); Hysteria, Dealer's Choice, My Night With Reg (Birmingham Rep); 5 @ 50, Charlie's Aunt, Hobson's Choice, Yerma (Royal Exchange Manchester); Us and Them, The Dead Eye Boy, Buried Alive (Hampstead); Madness of George III (West Yorkshire Playhouse/Birmingham Rep); Office (Edinburgh); For Alan Ayckbourn at Stephen Joseph Theatre Scarborough: Dear Uncle, Carmen, Awaking Beauty, Mr A's Amazing Maze Plays, Life of Riley. West End credits include: The Rivals, Rainman, Absurd Person Singular, Duet for One, Honour, Glorious, Great Balls of Fire, Some Girl(s), High Society, Rosencrantz And Guildenstern Are Dead, Kindertransport, Twelfth Night, Abigail's Party, And Then There Were None, What The Butler Saw, Iolanthe, The Mikado, Yeoman Of The Guard, The Letter and Pretending to be Me.

Steve Mayo Sound Designer

The Amazing Vancetti Sisters (Tristan Bates); Midnight Your Time, Dusk Rings A Bell and Nicked (HighTide Festival); Incoming (HighTide Festival/Latitude Festival); Lidless (E4 Underbelly, Edinburgh/Trafalgar Studios); Flesh and Blood & Fish and Fowl (Pit Theatre, Barbican, Associate Sound Designer); Flyboy is alone again this Christmas (Pit Theatre, Barbican); Our Share of Tomorrow (Edinburgh 10/York Theatre Royal); Cabaret Simon (Pit Theatre, Barbican); The Line (Arcola Theatre); Public Property (Trafalgar Studios); Ordinary Dreams (Trafalgar Studios); Muhmah, Guardians, Fixer (HighTide Festival 2009); Well (Apollo Theatre); Sh*t M*x (Trafalgar Studios); I Caught Crabs in Walberswick (HighTide/Bush Theatre/Edinburgh); Stovepipe (HighTide/National Theatre/Bush Theatre); Fight Face (Lyric Studio/Decibel Festival, Manchester); Lie of the Land, Lough/Rain (Edinburgh/Arcola Theatre/York Playhouse); Hangover Square (Finborough Theatre); Absolutely Frank (Queen's Theatre Hornchurch); Snowbound (Trafalgar Studios); Jack and the Beanstalk (Barbican Theatre); Romeo and Juliet (BAC); Weightless, You Were After Poetry, Lyre and Ned & Sharon (HighTide Festival 2007); Future/Perfect (Soho Theatre); Eden's Empire (Finborough Theatre); Miniaturists (Arcola); Mythomania (White Bear Theatre); Tale of Two Cities, Cinderella (G.S.M.D); Dr Foster (Menier Chocolate Factory); Silence (Arcola).

Composition: The Amazing Vancetti Sisters (Tristan Bates); Breathing Corpses, Soft Armour (Theatre Souk); Love & Money (Arts Ed); Guardians, Fixer (HighTide Festival 2009); Simpatico (Old Red Lion); Absolutely Frank (Queen's Theatre).

Watford Palace Theatre...

is a local theatre with a national reputation.

The creative hub at the heart of Watford, the Palace engages people through commissioning, creating and presenting high-quality theatre, and developing audiences, artists and communities through exciting opportunities to participate. Contributing to the identity of Watford and Hertfordshire, the Palace enriches people's lives, increases pride in the town, and raises the profile of the area. The beautiful 600-seat Edwardian Palace Theatre is a Grade II listed building, busy with live performances and film screenings seven days a week, offering world-class art to the tens of thousands of people visiting the Theatre each year.

The quality of work on stage and beyond is central to the Theatre's ethos. Recently, the Palace has enjoyed critical acclaim for its productions of Alan Ayckbourn's **Time Of My Life** (2011), Gary Owen's **Mrs Reynolds and the Ruffian** (2010, TMA Best New Play nomination) and Neil Simon's **Brighton Beach Memoirs** (2010, TMA Best Supporting Performance in a Play nomination).

Work created at Watford Palace Theatre regularly tours nationally. Recent co-productions include Tanika Gupta's **Great Expectations** with English Touring Theatre, **The Human Comedy** with the Opera Group and the Young Vic (nominated for the Evening Standard award for Best Musical), Marks and Gran's **Von Ribbentrop's Watch** with Oxford Playhouse, Jack Thorne's **Bunny** with nabokov (Edinburgh Fringe First 2010) and **Stick Man** with Scamp which continues to tour nationally and internationally.

The Palace has commissioned and is producing new plays with a range of exciting writers including Julian Mitchell's **Family Business** (2011) and Charlotte Keatley's **Our Father** (2012).

Projects such as **Windrush** (2010), **Hello, Mister Capello** (2010) and **Milestones** (2008) have brought together the creativity of Watford's diverse communities. These build on the regular programme of Palace and Hertfordshire County Youth Theatres, adult workshops, backstage tours, community choir and extensive work with schools.

A year in numbers...
- Reaching a total of 180,000 people
- Over 16,000 participatory sessions
- 177,000 unique website visits
- A pantomime attended by over 25,000 visitors
- More than 330 artists supported
- Visits generate over £1.2m of spending in the local economy
- Over 300 performances and 250 film screenings
- More than a dozen productions produced or co-produced
- Productions seen in more than 60 towns and cities across the UK

Watford Palace Theatre Creative Associates

Watford Palace Theatre extends the ambition and reach of its work through partnership projects and by offering developmental resources to the following Resident Companies and Creative Associates:

Resident Companies

Rifco Arts, a theatre company producing new writing celebrating British Asian culture

nabokov, a new writing theatre company from the Eastern region

Creative Associates

Charlotte Keatley, an internationally acclaimed playwright best known for her hit play My Mother Said I Never Should

Gary Owen, an award-winning playwright whose work has been successfully produced nationally

Kate Flatt, an acclaimed international choreographer living in Watford and working around the world

The Opera Group, producing and touring quality music theatre and opera

Scamp Theatre, producers for the Eastern region specialising in work for young people

Stacey Gregg, an emerging young playwright with a distinctive voice

Work created at and with Watford Palace Theatre regularly tours nationally. Productions you may have seen recently include:

Bunny
by Jack Thorne, a Fringe First-winning production in association with nabokov and the Mercury Colchester, which has toured nationally and played at London's Soho Theatre and in New York

Street Scene
Music by Kurt Weill, book by Elmer Rice, lyrics by Langston Hughes, co-produced with The Opera Group and the Young Vic, which won the Evening Standard award for Best Musical

Friend or Foe
by Michael Morpurgo, co-produced with Scamp Theatre

Britain's Got Bhangra
conceived and written by Pravesh Kumar, music by Sumeet Chopra, lyrics by Dougal Irvine, co-produced with Rifco Arts and Warwick Arts Centre

Young Pretender
by E V Crowe, co-produced with nabokov and Hull Truck Theatre in association with Mercury Colchester

Dusk Rings a Bell
by Stephen Belber, co-produced with HighTide Festival Theatre

Stickman
from the book by Julia Donaldson, co-produced with Scamp, which has toured internationally and played at London's Soho Theatre and the Edinburgh Festival

Great Expectations
by Charles Dickens, adapted by Tanika Gupta, co-produced with English Touring Theatre

Songs From A Hotel Bedroom
by Kate Flatt and Peter Rowe, music by Kurt Weill, co-produced with Segue and the New Wolsey Theatre and co-commissioned by ROH2 at the Royal Opera House

The Human Comedy
from an original story by William Saroyan, book by William Dumaresq with music by Galt MacDermot, co-produced with the Young Vic and The Opera Group

Von Ribbentrop's Watch
a new play by Laurence Marks and Maurice Gran, co-produced with Oxford Playhouse

My Hamlet with Linda Marlowe
an international partnership led by the Palace and NFA International Arts and Culture with Fingers Theatre, Tbilisi

The Lion's Face
a new opera from poet Glyn Maxwell and composer Elena Langer, co-produced with The Opera Group and Brighton Dome & Festival

www.watfordpalacetheatre.co.uk

Be Part of Watford Palace Theatre

Circle Membership
Enjoy an even more special relationship with Watford Palace by becoming a Circle Member.

Palace Circle £20 (£30 for two people with the same address)
- 10% off top price tickets
- 20% off 'Palace Tuesdays'
- Priority brochure mailing
- Regular Circle Newsletter
- No charge for postage on tickets bought by phone
- No exchange fee when changing tickets to another performance of the same show

Directors' Circle £175
All Palace Circle benefits plus
- Private backstage tours
- Acknowledgement in our show programmes
- Invitations to special events with artists working on productions

Corporate Membership Club
Join to enable your company to share our success whilst enjoying an extensive range of benefits. Introductory membership costs £500 +VAT per annum.

Sponsorship
Supporting Watford Palace offers your company the opportunity to be associated with a local theatre with a national reputation. We develop successful, mutually rewarding, tailored packages to suit your company's needs and CSR commitments.

Corporate Hire & Training
Watford Palace is the ideal place to host your business event, and can provide unique spaces for meetings, conferences and AGMs. We are able to offer exciting training opportunities tailored to the specific needs of your business. Using theatre-based skills for training is an ideal way to add something different to your staff development.

Donations and Legacies
As a local charity we welcome donations of any size, which go directly to support the work of the theatre and to maintain our listed building. You can donate online on our website or in person at the Box Office. Alternatively, a legacy or endowment can make a huge difference to the future of the Palace.

For further details please contact the Development Manager, on 01923 257472 or email development@watfordpalacetheatre.co.uk

Oxford Playhouse is a theatre for everyone

OP
OXFORD
PLAYHOUSE

Oxford Playhouse and its **Burton Taylor Studio** present and produce a wide range of live performance. The programme includes the best of British and international drama, family shows, contemporary dance and music, student and amateur shows, comedy, lectures and poetry.

The Playhouse has **Shared Experience** as its resident company and hosts Artists in Residence **Idle Motion, Walker Park, Michael Gabriel** and **The Opera Group**. It also presents **Playhouse Plays Out**, an on-going series of off-site shows which happen at varying locations across Oxfordshire.

The Playhouse's Learning team works with over 15,000 people each year through post show discussions, workshops, work experience, two resident young people's theatre companies, **Spotlight**, a group for over 60s and numerous holiday schemes.

Oxford Playhouse has been steadily increasing its producing arm, and in 2011 produced seven shows, including; a co-production of **Brontë** with Shared Experience which toured nationally, a new small-scale production of **The Wright Brothers** by David Hastings, which premiered at the Singapore Arts Festival before playing at the Edinburgh Fringe Festival in August, **Paterson Joseph's** new play **Sancho – An Act of Remembrance**, which premiered in the Burton Taylor Studio in September, and three Christmas shows; a revival of **Bath Time** playing Bristol Tobacco Factory throughout December, **Dear Father Christmas**, a new show for children under six, written and directed by Helen Eastman, that will premiere in the Burton Taylor Studio, and its annual pantomime, which this year is **Mother Goose**.

In 2012 the Playhouse will co-produce a new Helen Edmundson play with **Shared Experience** about Mary Shelley, a production of Dick King-Smith's **The Crowstarver** with Theatre Alibi and **Animal Farm** by the resident young people's theatre company, **16|22**.

Recent credits include: **One Small Step** (which was written by one of the Playhouse's stage door keepers, David Hastings, and has now been seen by 26,500 people in 20 different countries), Laurence Marks and Maurice Gran's **Von Ribbentrop's Watch**, in association with Watford Palace Theatre, a co-production with Theatre Alibi of Graham Greene's **The Ministry of Fear**; and its 2010 Christmas productions, **Cinderella** and **Bath Time**, a devised participative play by Toby Hulse for children under five.

For more information on Oxford Playhouse please visit www.oxfordplayhouse.com or contact Producer Michelle Knight at michelle.knight@oxfordplayhouse.com

You can follow the theatre on Facebook or on Twitter @OxfordPlayhouse

OXFORD PLAYHOUSE

SUPPORTERS

Support us and invest in our future

Without the generous support of our core funders, individual donors, sponsors, volunteers and audiences, Oxford Playhouse would not be here. Thank you for your support!

At Oxford Playhouse we are passionate about what we do and hope that you are too. By coming to the Playhouse, you help to keep the theatre thriving. If you can, please consider making a gift to support our future. We are a charity and each year we need to raise over £200,000 from charitable sources.

A gift to the Playhouse will help us to safeguard the strong artistic programme, develop our Learning and Community work and keep improving the building to make it as welcoming as possible.

There are a number of ways you can help:

– Make a gift to our fundraising campaign which you can now do online
– Set up a regular gift by standing order to provide vital on-going support
– Remember Oxford Playhouse in your will
– Talk to your company about how they can get involved

For further details, please look out for our leaflets in the foyer or contact the Development Office on 01865 305315 or development.office@oxfordplayhouse.com or visit www.oxfordplayhouse.com/supportus

Oxford Playhouse gratefully acknowledges the support of its core funders and support from:

Supported by
**ARTS COUNCIL
ENGLAND**

UNIVERSITY OF
OXFORD

LEISURE

OXFORD
CITY
COUNCIL

SUPPORTED BY
**OXFORDSHIRE
COUNTY COUNCIL**
Cultural Services

01865 305305
www.oxfordplayhouse.com

For Oxford Playhouse

Ashley Bale	Chief Electrician
Amy Elkins	Ticket Office Assistant
Charlie Field	Programme Manager
Claire Begley	Assistant Bar Manager
Costa Cambanakis	Deputy Chief Electrician
David Golder	Stage Door Keeper
Eliza Fraser	Bar Assistant
Erin Crivelli	Marketing Manager
Gemma Summerfield	Front of House Manager
Graeme Everist	Finance Manager
Heather Wright	Catering Manager
Hester Bond	Learning Officer
Jane Hornsby	Administrative Assistant
Jo Noble	Youth Theatre Director
Jo Osborne	Development Manager
Jocelyn English	Ticket Office Assistant
Jonny Bell	Maintenance Technician
Krystyna Chawluk	Ticket Office Administrator
Laura Bradley	Assistant Ticket Office Manager
Laura Choules	Assistant Electrician
Laura Sherwood	Ticket Office Assistant
Lauren Caddick	Assistant Ticket Office Manager
Linda Hickman	Finance Officer
Lisa Wood	Marketing and Digital Media Officer
Madeleine Vose	Learning and Community Manager
Madeleine Woolgar	Marketing and Press Officer
Maisy Ash	Community Engagement Officer
Mary Osborn	Ticket Office Assistant
Michelle Dickson	Theatre Director
Michelle Knight	Producer
Naomi Webb	University Drama Officer
Nathan Grassi	Ticket Office Assistant
Nick Jordan	Ticket Office Manager
Phil Smith	ICT Manager
Polly Cole	Deputy Director
Rachel Green	Development Officer
Rachel Joubert	Assistant Front of House Manager
Rebecca Tay	Assistant Front of House Manager
Richard Gladstone	Administration Volunteer
Richard Willoughby	Head Stage Door Keeper
Robert Bristow	Burton Taylor Studio Manager
Robert Morton	Bar Manager
Russell Souch	Marketing and Information Officer
Simon Ayloff	Deputy Stage Manager
Stewart Smith	Operations Manager
Stuart Allen	Assistant Producer
Tim Boyd	Technical Manager
Tom Howard	Ticket Office Assistant
Zeb Turner - Johnson	Technical Stage Manager

For Watford Palace Theatre

Boards of Directors
Martin Baker
Jacqueline Boast
Alex Bottom
Jim Cooke (Cafe & Bars)
George Derbyshire
Kim Grant
Paul Harris
Beverley Jullien
Sneha Khilay
Melody Laffy
David Lloyd
Katharine McMahon
Alok Mitra
Alastair Robertson (Chair)
Jenny Topper

Artistic Director and Chief Executive
Brigid Larmour
Executive Director
Mathew Russell

Operations
Programme & Projects Manager
Stephanie Hay
Administrator/PA to the Directors
Barry Moules
Buildings Manager
Steve Burke
Maintenance Technician
Brian Penston
Finance Manager
Andrew Phillips
Finance Officer
Katrina Tepper

Participation
Head of Participation
Kirsten Hutton
Resident Director (Participation)
James Williams
Participation Co-ordinator
Tom Harland
Participation Assistant (Placement)
George Pearce

Production
Head of Production
Matt Ledbury
Head of Electrics
Richmond Rudd
Deputy Head of Electrics
Francis Johnstone
Technician
Daniel Frost
Stage Technician
Chris Taylor
Company Stage Manager
Peter Jamieson
Wardrobe Supervisor
Holly White
Head of Construction
Tip Pargeter
Construction Assistant
James Weatherby
Work Experience Placement
Liam Summerfield

Communications
Marketing and Press Manager
Emily Lincoln
Audience Development Officer
Mellissa Flowerdew-Clarke
Promotions and Distribution Assistant
Rebecca Boyce
Sales & Membership Manager
Claire Nickless
Sales & Membership Assistants
Caitriona Gill, Beth Ryan, Gemma Marks
Customer Services Manager
Amy Platt
Casual Front of House Managers
Paul Mead, Natalie Johnson
Development Manager
Lynne Misner
Cafe and Bars Manager
Ross Wilday
Cafe Staff
Rachel Leaver, Frances Lyons

Follow us:

Supported by

**ARTS COUNCIL
ENGLAND**

FAMILY BUSINESS

Julian Mitchell

FAMILY BUSINESS

OBERON BOOKS
LONDON

WWW.OBERONBOOKS.COM

First published in 2011 by Oberon Books Ltd
521 Caledonian Road, London N7 9RH
Tel: +44 (0) 20 7607 3637 / Fax: +44 (0) 20 7607 3629
e-mail: info@oberonbooks.com
www.oberonbooks.com

Copyright © Julian Mitchell 2011

Julian Mitchell is hereby identified as author of this play in
accordance with section 77 of the Copyright, Designs and Patents
Act 1988. The author has asserted his moral rights.

All rights whatsoever in this play are strictly reserved and
application for performance etc. should be made before
commencement of rehearsal to United Agents, 12-26 Lexington
Street, London W1F 0LE. No performance may be given unless
a licence has been obtained, and no alterations may be made in
the title or the text of the play without the author's prior written
consent.

This book is sold subject to the condition that it shall not by way
of trade or otherwise be circulated without the publisher's consent
in any form of binding or cover or circulated electronically other
than that in which it is published and without a similar condition
including this condition being imposed on any subsequent
purchaser.

A catalogue record for this book is available from the British
Library.

ISBN: 978-1-84943-095-1

Cover credit
Design: Cog Design
Photograph: Chris Gloag
Background: David Toase/Getty Images

Printed and bound by CPI Group (UK) Ltd, Croydon, CR0 4YY.

Characters

SOLOMON

WILLIAM

TOM

JANE

KATE

HUGO

ACT ONE

The scene is a converted barn on the Welsh borders, with a view of the Black Mountains. There is a garden, mostly paved, but with roses.

Act One is indoors.

It is afternoon.

WILLIAM is sixty-seven, a sharp, quick-witted Englishman in a wheelchair. He looks off to make sure no one can see him, then raises himself very carefully from the chair, and stands a moment, swaying. He takes a step, wobbles, has to clutch at a table. He stands up straight again, tries another step, but his balance is wrong. He curses silently, then makes his way back to the chair, holding on to the table. He sits. After a moment he wheels himself over to the window.

SOLOMON comes in with a glass of water and a pill on a tray. He is African, about fifty, but with a completely RP English accent.

SOLOMON: Lifting your eyes unto the hills?

WILLIAM: My delectable mountains. Delectable, at least, when the rain clears away.

SOLOMON: Heaven always comes with ifs and buts.

He offers the pill. WILLIAM makes a face but takes it.

SOLOMON: I can't remember – Is Hugo vegan or vegetarian these days?

WILLIAM: Depends how annoying he wants to be.

SOLOMON: Better make it vegan, then.

WILLIAM: Valerie spoiled him, that's his trouble. Had too much attention as a child. Now, as he can't get it by being exceptionally clever or nice or beautiful, he gets it by being peculiarly irritating.

SOLOMON: What insight.

WILLIAM: Am I becoming a bore?

SOLOMON: *(Tease.)* Becoming?

WILLIAM: Life is so stupidly organized. By the time you know something worth knowing everyone thinks you're too old to know anything at all.

Mobile phone goes.

WILLIAM: If it's a man in Calcutta, tell him to get stuffed. With a Bombay duck.

SOLOMON answers.

SOLOMON: Hello? Oh, hello, Martin. He's right here. Hold on.

(Taking phone to WILLIAM.) Martin Phillips.

WILLIAM: Oh, good.

SOLOMON: Now don't excite yourself.

WILLIAM: *(To phone.)* Martin, what have you found?

(Listens.) There was no formal agreement, no, but the two properties have shared the spring for hundreds if not thousands of –

(Listens.) But he did it so sneakily! Taking advantage of my absence under the surgeon's knife to –

(Listens.) But he should have consulted me first! Surely?

(Listens.) Well, I'm disappointed. Very. Are you absolutely positive there's nothing –

(Listens.) Well, thank you. Thank you, Martin.

(Switches off.) For nothing.

He hands the phone back to SOLOMON.

WILLIAM: Lawyers!

SOLOMON: Told you.

WILLIAM: But it was such a mean, cowardly thing to do. I'm not letting Prichard get away with it.

SOLOMON: His borehole was running dry, his bullocks were thirsty, you hadn't been here for three weeks –

WILLIAM: He was hoping I'd die, of course, and no one would notice he'd quietly filched my water.

SOLOMON: There's plenty for everyone.

WILLIAM: *(Glowering.)* Not the point.

SOLOMON: *(Casual.)* Valerie liked Prichard. He brought her duck eggs.

WILLIAM: Duck eggs!

(Anxious.) She really was happy here, wasn't she?

SOLOMON: Most of the time.

WILLIAM: I did want her not to be so anxious.

SOLOMON: It was part of the illness.

(Frown.) I was going to make Hugo a cauliflower cheese, but if he's vegan –

WILLIAM: Do your risotto primavera.

SOLOMON: But it's not spring.

WILLIAM: It's always spring in the freezer. Hugo can add parmesan or not, according to his conscience.

(Turns away, fretting.) Bloody lawyers. Now the hills have lost their lustre.

He wheels himself across to the other window and stares out.

SOLOMON: The plains any better?

WILLIAM: No.

(Beat.) She really was happy here?

SOLOMON: Happier than anywhere else.

WILLIAM: *(Going back to the hill view.)* I always wanted hills. It was so flat round Stratford. I could never show off the gears on my bike.

SOLOMON: Three speed?

WILLIAM: Five!

SOLOMON: Drop handlebars?

WILLIAM: Of course. And a racing saddle. The higher you could get your arse in the air –

SOLOMON laughs.

WILLIAM: Jimmy Spooner, whose father was a chemist, so they were richer than us – Have I told you this?

SOLOMON: Don't know yet.

WILLIAM: I forget who I've told what. Everything blurs after anaesthetic.

SOLOMON: It's three months now.

WILLIAM: Things still aren't as clear as they used to be.

SOLOMON: Are they ever?

WILLIAM: Of course it may just be general decay.

SOLOMON: Now, now.

WILLIAM: *(Beat.)* Jimmy Spooner could get his saddle four inches higher than anyone else. His arse was practically in the clouds. He was supposed to be my friend but I hated him.

SOLOMON: No, you didn't tell me.

WILLIAM: Poor Jimmy. Left school at sixteen to work behind his father's counter. So bored he'd got the cosmetics assistant pregnant by the end of the year.

SOLOMON: Careless. In a chemist.

WILLIAM: It wasn't like today, shameless ticklers in full view. Old Spooner was a Wesleyan. Wouldn't sell contraceptives to a woman unless she had a doctor's prescription.

SOLOMON: Did Jimmy marry the girl?

WILLIAM: She wasn't a girl. She was almost forty. But yes. Had to. This was Stratford.

SOLOMON: No more cycle rides for him, then.

WILLIAM: No. Died at fifty-three of lack of exercise and boredom. If you didn't escape from Stratford, you just slumbered your way to death.

SOLOMON: You shouldn't talk like that about your birthplace. It's where your soul arrived on earth.

WILLIAM: Is that what the missionaries taught you?

SOLOMON: Didn't need anyone teaching me. It's what everyone knows. And you had Shakespeare.

WILLIAM: A shrine is a bad place to grow up. You're so busy fleecing the pilgrims, you lose all faith in the saint. And the fact that the old poop in the church asked that no one should dig him up –

SOLOMON: That's disrespectful, William. He brought you so much business.

WILLIAM: True. But if yet another loony wanted to prove that the plays were written by Agatha Christie or Jeffrey Archer, we'd have sold him spades and pickaxes along with mugs with the sainted poop's head on –

SOLOMON: Mugs for mugs.

WILLIAM: – half-timbered pottery cottages, Anne Hathaway tea towels – pokerwork texts from the plays – God, have I invented it, or were there really mouth organs inscribed 'If music be the food of love, play on'?

SOLOMON: You invented it. Didn't you?

WILLIAM: Not sure.

SOLOMON: He brought you a theatre.

WILLIAM: Oh, we locals never went there. Except the mayor. He had to go, first play of the season, in his chain and hat. But he didn't go again. Not voluntarily. Not paying for his ticket. The plays were like the mugs – strictly for tourists. What Stratford liked was a nice brass band. The council would stump up for that. Not for the theatre, not for years. If I hadn't been doing *Hamlet* for O-Levels I wouldn't have gone myself. But then *Hamlet* – not on the page, not in a set book, but on stage! When you're fifteen! I thought I *was* Hamlet. Went back on my own, three times.

(Glum.) I suppose I'm Prospero now. Or Lear. Oh, I do hope I'm not Lear.

He feels the button on his open-necked shirt and pretends to choke.

SOLOMON: You don't have the beard for Lear. You're more Polonius.

WILLIAM: *(Pleased.)* Oh? I've always thought Polonius rather witty.

A car can be heard arriving off.

WILLIAM: Ah! Jane. Bet you. Always likes to get her word in before anyone else.

SOLOMON: *(At window.)* It's Tom. Swimmers! Wish I was still as slim as that.

WILLIAM: *(Suddenly anxious.)* Solomon – is this whole thing a mistake?

SOLOMON: Soon see.

He opens the door for TOM, who is thirty-seven, very fit, slim and athletic. He has a wrapped bottle of champagne.

SOLOMON: Tom! Hi!

TOM: Hi, Solomon! Hi, Dad! Happy Birthday!

He gives him the champagne.

WILLIAM: Please don't say Hi, it's so American.

TOM: Aloha, then!

WILLIAM: What's wrong with 'hello'?

TOM: *(To SOLOMON.)* He's feeling OK again, then! Straight into the attack!

SOLOMON: Family always sharpens him up. Can I get you something?

TOM: A glass of water would be nice.

WILLIAM: I think we still have some water left, don't we, Solomon?

SOLOMON makes a face at him and goes.

TOM: What does that mean?

WILLIAM: Oh, my ancient British neighbour, Evan Prichard, the bastard, his borehole started drying up, so he waited till I was in hospital then put a pump in the spring we share, and now he's drawing off most of my water. As soon as I can get up there, I'm going to poison the spring. Then he'll wake up one morning to find all his bullocks dead.

TOM: Won't that be a bit obvious?

WILLIAM: I can't hang about, Tom. Don't know how long I've got.

TOM: How are you? Really?

WILLIAM: As you see. Legless. Without benefit of drink.

TOM: How long are you going to be stuck in that thing?

WILLIAM: This 'thing', as you call it is very high-tech. Titanium. The Rolls Royce of wheelchairs.

He demonstrates.

TOM: Wow.

WILLIAM: But I may die in it.

TOM: *(Shocked.)* I thought the doctors –

WILLIAM: Oh, my life expectancy is the same as for anyone else my age. But I may be so overcome by the love and affection of you children, that I choke to death on my birthday cake this very afternoon.

TOM: Is that a threat or a promise?

WILLIAM laughs.

WILLIAM: Actually, I'm only in this because I haven't got my balance back yet. In any sense, you'll say, so let me say it first. Getting on and off the loo – it's like climbing an overhang. A grab here, a grab there –

TOM: You'll be up in the hills again soon.

WILLIAM: No false comfort, thank you.

TOM: I'd have come before, but Jane said by the time I arrived it would be all over, and –

WILLIAM: It'd be all over with me, you mean?

TOM: No, no. The operation would be over and –

WILLIAM: I *might* be dead.

TOM: She didn't say anything at all about you being dead.

WILLIAM: Were you very disappointed?

TOM: Dad – She said there was nothing I could do here. And as there was a lot I could do out there –

WILLIAM: Do you know how I knew I wasn't going to die? This time, anyway? When I came back from the High Dependency Unit, I looked at the pictures on the wall of my room and saw bed upon bed of ghastly Edwardian lupins.

TOM: What's wrong with lupins?

WILLIAM: It was like being in a garden of remembrance. So I said to Solomon, for God's sake, take those down and bring me in my John Martin illustrations to *Paradise Lost*. Remember them?

TOM: Umm –

WILLIAM: Black and white prints of heaven and hell. And Solomon said, Are you sure? And I said, Of course I'm sure. And he laughed and said, Not bothered about the afterlife, then? And we both knew I was going to be all right.

TOM: Yes, well, while you were rearranging your pictures, the rest of us were worrying about the world economy.

WILLIAM: Word of its sluggishness did reach me. Through the anaesthetic fog.

SOLOMON comes back in with a glass of water for TOM.

SOLOMON: Here you are, Tom. The water of life.

WILLIAM: From my raped and pillaged spring.

TOM: Thanks.

WILLIAM: Tom's about to tell us how the recession has forced him to recede.

SOLOMON: Oh? Coral Paradise not on target?

TOM: Is anywhere at the moment?

WILLIAM: Mr Chung must have a few billions left, surely?

TOM: Not a bean.

They both look at him, serious now.

TOM: Never had one to begin with, it turns out. There was lots of fancy bamboo scaffolding, and behind it, noughts beyond number. But nothing behind them.

SOLOMON shakes his head.

TOM: Except a cat's cradle of interlocking companies, all passing the absence of money to each other at compound interest.

WILLIAM: When did this come out?

TOM: Two months ago. After he drove himself off the end of an unfinished motorway bridge in Shanghai.

WILLIAM: Shows a certain style.

TOM: They say he'd have gone to prison for something like seventy-five years. Plus life.

WILLIAM: A lot to look forward to, then.

TOM: The thing is, we've almost finished the village. The generator's up and running, we've built a new jetty for the diving boats, the huts are all done, and the dining room/kitchen, except for its thatch. The only other thing left is the airstrip.

SOLOMON: I thought you had an airstrip. On the side of a hill. You said how you landed uphill and took off down.

TOM: We do. And guests would have loved it. It's perfectly safe, but they'd have felt like explorers, right at the edge of the civilized world.

WILLIAM: Pushing the boundaries, but having all the injections first. Breathless adventure without real danger. First class, Tom.

TOM: But then – with no warning at all – the Airport Authority said we had to have a flat strip. And as the island is the tip of an extinct volcano – Chung said to leave it to him, and he went off to bribe the head of the Airport Authority, only he turned out to be a born-again Christian, and either Chung didn't offer him enough, or –

WILLIAM: You can never offer a Christian enough. Conscience doth make cashiers of them all.

SOLOMON claps, but TOM doesn't get it.

TOM: Anyway, he took offence and – Well, eventually Chung said, the hell with it, order the JCBs back in, so I did, and we started work on the only flat place on the island. I had to give him a slightly larger chunk of the future profit –

WILLIAM: Another chunk for the Chink!

SOLOMON: William!

WILLIAM: Sorry.

TOM: The strip's half done now. But since Chung –

WILLIAM: Went over the edge.

SOLOMON: Stop it!

TOM: I couldn't pay to take the JCBs away again now, even if I wanted. Which of course I don't. I want to get the place finished. But all our accounts are frozen.

WILLIAM: On a tropical island!

TOM: And the receivers are pretending it's worth only a third of its real value.

(Real frustration.) We have ten miles of virgin coral reef, the clearest water you've ever seen, fantastic fish, some of them not yet officially recorded –

WILLIAM: I read the brochure.

TOM: I'm working on a new one. Coral Paradise as the new, the virgin, the undiscovered country.

WILLIAM: You can't say that.

TOM: Why not?

WILLIAM sighs.

SOLOMON: It's from *Hamlet*. To be or not to be.

TOM doesn't understand.

WILLIAM: To be or not to be is about whether or not to commit suicide. The undiscovered country is one from which no traveller returns. As Mr Chung has just demonstrated. Unless the suicide was fake.

TOM: Oh.

SOLOMON: So what happens now?

WILLIAM: Yes, must Coral Paradise be lost, too?

TOM: Well – There's not only the strip to finish, and the dining hall roof, there's the local staff to train – marketing. But I still want to open in time for Christmas.

WILLIAM: Christmas Corals! How much?

TOM: Peanuts. Two million.

SOLOMON: *(Beat.)* Dollars?

TOM: Pounds.

WILLIAM raises an eyebrow.

TOM: But I can't get a single bank in Europe or America or China even to let me make a pitch. They say it doesn't fit with their current parameters.

WILLIAM: Bankers' language has always been deplorable. It's because they don't want anyone to understand what they're saying. Because they don't understand it themselves.

Beat.

How long before an investor might see a return on his money?

TOM: Well – There's a big drop in general tourism at the moment, of course. But reef-diving is a very special area,

I don't think we're going to suffer too much. And Coral Paradise being new, and so incredibly exciting –

WILLIAM: You don't have to keep selling it to me.

Beat.

When you decided to strike out on your own, Tom, to leave the shelter of the company, you had my blessing. Not because you were bloody useless at the travel business, as your brother and sisters claimed –

TOM laughs quite bitterly.

WILLIAM: – but because you reminded me of myself when your mother and I started up. We thought we'd seen something no one else had, and went after it.

Beat.

But two million pounds – that's quite a visionary number of peanuts.

TOM: I was wondering –

(Very hesitant.) Mum's trust.

WILLIAM: Yes?

TOM: Holds 49 per cent of the shares.

WILLIAM: Yes?

TOM: She left them for us.

WILLIAM: Indeed.

TOM: Well –

Sound of another car arriving. SOLOMON goes to the window.

WILLIAM: Ah, someone else after money, I expect.

SOLOMON: It's Jane.

WILLIAM: Of course! We'll talk about it later, Tom. When everyone's here.

SOLOMON is opening the door for JANE.

SOLOMON: Hi, Jane!

JANE comes on, giving him a quick formal smile. She is two years older than TOM, in a tweed skirt and jacket. She stops short, seeing TOM.

JANE: *(Annoyed.)* Tom! You beat me to it!

TOM: Hi!

JANE kisses WILLIAM.

JANE: Daddy! Happy birthday!

She hands him a small parcel in gaudy paper.

WILLIAM: What's this?

JANE: It's from the twins. Susie made the present. Jessica painted the wrapping paper.

WILLIAM just looks at it.

JANE: Here – let me.

She quickly opens the parcel and hands him a pillbox made of shells.

WILLIAM: It's – it's –

SOLOMON: It's lovely, Jane.

He gets another quick polite smile.

WILLIAM: But what is it?

JANE: A pillbox.

(To others.) When Susie heard that Gramps was having to take a lot of pills – We couldn't afford abroad this year, so we went to Broad Haven instead – it's so lovely there when the sun shines – and Susie was collecting shells, and she said, What shall I do with them, Mummy, I know, I'll make a box for Gramps's pills! Wasn't that sweet?

WILLIAM: Sweet.

SOLOMON: Very sweet.

WILLIAM: *(A threat.)* Now I shall think of her every time I have to take a bloody pill.

JANE: I'm sorry I'm late –

WILLIAM: You're not.

JANE: – but there's a gymkhana tomorrow and Susie fell off this morning and broke the peak of her riding cap, so I had to go and get her another, and then the traffic on the M32 –

(Finally bringing herself to acknowledge his presence.) How are you, Solomon?

SOLOMON: Fine, thanks.

JANE: *(Going to window.)* This place is such heaven.

SOLOMON: Tea, Jane?

JANE: Would make it perfect!

SOLOMON: Heaven is never perfect.

JANE and TOM look at him in surprise.

SOLOMON: It's like a garden. There's always something to do. Weeding. Watering. Pruning. Then maybe it would be better if you grassed over this bed here and made one there instead. And what about a fountain? I've always thought a fountain would look good in the rose garden.

JANE: *(Taken aback.)* Yes, well, I –

SOLOMON: The changes you make don't make the garden better or worse. But they do make it different. It would be so dull if heaven was always the same.

JANE: I'm afraid I haven't thought about it. I was just – you know –

SOLOMON: *(Smile.)* I like your new hair. When did you cut it?

JANE: Oh – last week.

TOM indicates to WILLIAM he thinks it a mistake.

SOLOMON: It's great. See what I mean? It was lovely before, but you changed it and look! It's still lovely!

WILLIAM: When you two have finished lovey-doveying each other –

SOLOMON laughs and goes.

JANE: *(To TOM.)* Solomon was so good when Daddy was ill. They let him sleep on a mattress on the floor of his room. Because if you have someone you know in the room with you, it helps you stay calm before an operation. And he was wonderful with Mummy. Never got cross with her. And she could be quite – quite –

WILLIAM: Infuriating.

JANE: Oh, but –

WILLIAM: I had to stop myself shouting at her sometimes. She'd ask you something – what day of the week it was, that sort of thing. You'd tell her, but two minutes later she'd ask the same thing again, and again two minutes after that, on and on, all morning and afternoon –

JANE: She couldn't help it. Poor Mummy.

TOM: What does Solomon do for fun? There isn't a pub for five miles.

WILLIAM: He's got me. I'm a laugh a minute. And he chooses the DVDs we watch. All very highbrow. Arthouse stuff. Currently we're doing Iranian cinema since 1979.

TOM: What happened in 1979?

WILLIAM: Come, come! The Islamic Revolution! Ayatollahs! Surely you remember?

TOM: Dad, I was one.

WILLIAM: Good Lord. Thought you'd been around much longer than that. It caused us terrible trouble. Hundreds of bookings cancelled, and the insurance people tried to maintain that the act of an ayatollah was the same as an act of God.

(Straight on, to JANE.) How's Bernard?

JANE: A little down still. He hardly dares go to his club, people are so mean to people in finance.

WILLIAM: Well –

TOM: Do you think he'd lend me a couple of million?

WILLIAM laughs shortly.

JANE: *(Ignoring that.)* This awful recession or depression or whatever it is – it would have to happen just as we're having to decide about the twins' education.

TOM: Oh?

JANE: *(Prepared and rehearsed.)* Three Ways has been fine up to now, you see, and Jessica's really very bright, but though she *is* clever, she's not top of the class, and Mrs Powell says she's actually a little lazy. She's always found it so easy to be ahead of Susie, you see. Susie's a darling, of course, but she's not the brightest of sparks, and Mrs Powell thinks that if Jess is to go to university – it's so difficult to get in nowadays, they want all As and A-stars – she needs the challenge of more competition. She thinks we ought to separate them for a while.

WILLIAM: They're – twelve?

JANE: Thirteen in October. We think the only solution for Jessie is a boarding school.

WILLIAM: You plan to send her away from home, just when a girl most needs her mother?

JANE: Well, of course, we'll miss her terribly, but if it's good for her in the long run –

WILLIAM: What happens to Susie?

JANE: Bernard says we must be fair. It wouldn't be right to send one of them away and not the other. And Susie – Bernard thought she might be dyslexic, so we went to a most expensive specialist –

WILLIAM: There's no other kind.

JANE: – and it turns out she can read when she wants to – *Pony Magazine*, she reads that cover to cover the moment it arrives – but she's just not interested in books. As such. She's the complete outdoor girl. So we thought, for her, a school where she can take her pony –

TOM: Are there such places?

WILLIAM: Oh, yes. The ponies can only do the simplest equations, of course. But then so can the girls.

JANE: *(Unconvincing laugh.)* What do you think, Daddy? I'll hate not having them at home, but I'll be able to give much more time to the business.

WILLIAM: Send them both to the local comprehensive.

JANE: But it's huge. And – and they'll come back with such dreadful accents.

WILLIAM: They'll soon lose them. I lost mine.

TOM: How much would it cost? Two girls at posh schools?

JANE: Well, that's just it, Tom. Unfortunately this recession began just as Bernard went independent, and –

WILLIAM laughs.

JANE: He wasn't to know.

WILLIAM: If financial advisers don't know, who does? And what are they for?

SOLOMON is coming on with tea for JANE.

SOLOMON: Here we are, Jane.

JANE: Oh, thank you.

WILLIAM: Solomon, Jane needs advice on the twins' education. Tell her about yours.

SOLOMON: Didn't have any till I got to England.

JANE: Was there no school in your – your –

SOLOMON: There was a school, yes. But it was firebombed before I could even start there.

JANE: Fire-bombed?

SOLOMON: There was a civil war. The rebels machine-gunned the kids as they ran out.

Silence.

WILLIAM: *(Gently.)* His brother was among them.

SOLOMON: *(Glare at WILLIAM.)* It's not something people generally want to hear about.

WILLIAM: *(Cheery.)* Jane wants me to pay for the twins to go to boarding schools.

JANE: I didn't say that! I –

WILLIAM: What did you think of yours?

SOLOMON: It was very –

(Hesitation.) Christian.

WILLIAM: Mr and Mrs Birlingham were very old-fashioned, you see. When they adopted Solomon, they decided to make a proper Englishman of him.

JANE: *(Polite.)* Our problems must seem very small to you, of course.

SOLOMON: Everything's relative. When I was seven I was strutting about with a Kalashnikov. Terrified. Now I worry about whether Hugo's vegan or vegetarian.

TOM: He wasn't eating cheese when he came to see me.

JANE: No. This new girlfriend of his – Chloe – she's absolutely fanatical.

WILLIAM: *(To SOLOMON.)* Jane wants Jessica to go to university. What do you think? Three years hanging around smoking pot and reading books?

SOLOMON: Sounds good to me.

JANE: It wasn't like that for me.

TOM laughs, jeeringly.

JANE: Perhaps I didn't know the right people. Or the wrong ones. I *worked.*

TOM: Oh, yes, Goody Two-shoes!

JANE: Mummy was so keen for me to do well. Having wanted so badly to go herself. If Grandpa hadn't died –

SOLOMON: She used to say that fifty times a day towards the end. If Daddy hadn't gone and died – When she couldn't make sense of anything else, she still knew she'd missed out. Like she wished she'd spent more time abroad, like William.

WILLIAM: *(Slightly cross.)* When Valerie and I set up the company we agreed to divide responsibilities. I don't think I'd have been very good at staying home and looking after you children.

JANE: But we hardly saw you. Then you'd suddenly turn up with a sack of presents like Father Christmas –

TOM: Yes, and more or less tip them out on the floor and tell us to divide them up among ourselves.

JANE: As though you were too busy to remember how many we were or which of us was which.

TOM: Then you shoved off back up the chimney to Laos or Lithuania or somewhere while we wondered what to do with them.

JANE: *(To TOM.)* Remember the alligator slippers?

TOM laughs.

JANE: *(To SOLOMON.)* They were made of real alligator skin. My toes curled up if I even looked at them. I thought they'd eat me.

SOLOMON laughs.

WILLIAM: What about the jade earrings? I brought those for you specially. And then you wouldn't wear them.

JANE: They didn't go with my eyes. You hadn't noticed what colour my eyes were.

Silence.

TOM: If it's Jane, she'll complain.

JANE shrugs, feeling she's made her point.

WILLIAM: *(To TOM.)* Did I fail you too?

TOM: You never came to my swimming competitions. Not that I was bothered.

JANE: *(Mocking.)* Not much you weren't!

WILLIAM: Oh, dear, I'm not sure I'm strong enough yet for a whole afternoon of filial reproaches.

JANE: *(Still cross.)* Why don't you want your grandchildren to have a decent education?

WILLIAM: I'm not against their education. Only against two perfectly ordinary, perfectly nice little girls being taught to think they're better than other people because they go to a private school and talk posh. It'll warp them for life.

SOLOMON: Would that by any chance be an old grammar school boy speaking from an ancient grudge?

WILLIAM: Very likely. I hated the way people didn't listen to what I said, only to the accent I said it in. Why I changed it.

SOLOMON: Making you a bit of a snob, too?

WILLIAM: It was more a commercial decision. I was spending most of my time with foreigners, who didn't have much grasp of the English social system, but could understand what was then the standard BBC accent better than my rural Warwickshire, tinged with urban Birmingham. Of course the BBC is now staffed entirely by people with incomprehensible local accents who –

KATE appears. She is late twenties, dressed very smart and young.

WILLIAM: Kate! Sweetheart! You're just in time to stop me being an insufferably churlish old man. Attacking the BBC when it's about the only good thing left in this country.

KATE: That does sound a *little* churlish.

She kisses him.

KATE: But it means you must be feeling better! Happy birthday!

TOM: How's things, Kate?

KATE: *(Kissing him.)* Exciting. Solomon!

She flings her arms round him and kisses him too. JANE doesn't like this. KATE does not kiss her.

KATE: Now – I've brought you a present, Dad.

WILLIAM: It's not a pillbox is it?

KATE: No, it's a brilliant wheeze for rocketing us out of the economic slowdown and zooming ahead of our rivals. Have you noticed how comedians are making pots of money out of bad taste jokes? Well, I've invented a bad taste tour of Britain.

JANE: For heaven's sake!

KATE: We start in Haringey.

TOM: Why Haringey?

KATE: So we can inspect the social services department. To see how they missed all the poor battered babies.

JANE: That's not funny.

KATE: We go on to Gloucester to visit the house of Frederick West. People love a multiple murderer.

WILLIAM laughs.

TOM: Where are you taking them for dinner? You get a duke when you go on Jane's art tours.

KATE: Mine get a duchess. Only she's very impoverished and lives in an unmodernised terrace cottage in Blackburn, surrounded by members of Al-Qaeda. She'll serve baked beans on toast, followed by treacle sponge from a tin, while she reminisces about the grand comradeship of people of all classes in the war. Next day we take the party through the Lake District.

JANE: Something nice to look at at last.

KATE: While it's still dark. We've got to get on to Sellafield.

WILLIAM laughs again.

KATE: Where we'll put on white suits to inspect the parts which tingle most with radiation. After a brisk dip in the radioactive sea, we take a short drive to Morecambe Sands where we join a party of Chinese cockle-pickers, just as the tide is beginning to come in.

JANE: This joke was not funny to begin with. It's now not funny at all.

KATE: Nearly finished. Just a three hour hold-up at Spaghetti Junction as we go on down to Swindon for a session in a call centre. You're not allowed home till you've sold fifty units of double glazing.

WILLIAM claps.

KATE: It'll be hugely popular. We'll offer a special discount for old Marxists, beached from the Sixties, rubbing their hands and saying I told you so. What do you think, Dad?

WILLIAM: I think you're a sweetheart.

JANE: Huh!

KATE: So does my fiancé.

SOLOMON: Another? So soon after the last?

WILLIAM: Number four, is it?

JANE: Five.

KATE sticks her tongue out at her.

WILLIAM: I'm all for people playing the field for a few years –

JANE: Daddy!

WILLIAM: When we're young, we're so vulnerable to – emotional error, let's call it. I certainly was. But you, Kate – you've been playing it long enough. Time you settled down.

KATE: *(Amused.)* I'm going to. Look!

She shows ring.

TOM: Wow! Real diamond?

KATE: Of course.

JANE: Very – very –

KATE: I think 'large' is the word you're looking for.

WILLIAM: *(Rather heavy.)* A rich fiancé? That's a breach with tradition, isn't it?

JANE: Better than that awful hairdresser person.

KATE: Warren was very nice. In some ways. But I washed him out of my hair the night I met Milo.

She doesn't see how WILLIAM reacts to the name.

KATE: You remember Milo Fanshawe when we were kids?

JANE: I don't think so.

KATE: I hadn't seen him for twenty something years. Not since we were in primary school together. But I recognized him at once by his very long nose. Taller now, of course. Very black hair, dreamy brown eyes – lovely ears with long lobes –

JANE: Really!

TOM laughs.

KATE: Oh, and he's tremendously clever. Only I'm so busy watching the way his lips move I can't concentrate on what he's saying, they're so –

SOLOMON: Finely chiselled?

She laughs.

KATE: Am I very Mills and Boon?

SOLOMON: You're not exactly Samuel Beckett.

TOM: What does this paragon of yours do with his long nose? What does he stick it into?

KATE: Computers. He's in charge of all the computers in his father's company.

The mobile phone goes.

KATE: *(Excited.)* They're the brewers.

TOM: Great! Free beer for all the brothers-in-law!

SOLOMON: *(On phone.)* Hello. Oh, Susie, how are you? No, she's here.

JANE: That child! She's always wanting something.

She goes to take the phone, but KATE gets to SOLOMON first.

KATE: Let me talk to her. Hello, darling! No, it's Kate. Your aunt Kate, silly. I've just got engaged, isn't it – Oh. Oh, dear. Yes, she's here. Hold on.

She hands the phone to JANE.

KATE: Something about the gymkhana tomorrow.

JANE: Don't say it's been cancelled. Susie?

SOLOMON: I think Kate's news calls for champagne.

WILLIAM thinks the opposite. He is in great confusion, but tries not to show it.

WILLIAM: It's wrong to have champagne before tea, surely?

SOLOMON: We can pretend it's still after lunch.

WILLIAM: But Hugo's not here.

SOLOMON: Oh, he's probably gone TT as well as vegan.

JANE: Have you looked in the cupboard?

KATE: He'll be here in a moment. I passed him on his bike as I came through the village. I gave him a wave, but he shook his fist at me.

JANE: No, no, the one in the tack-room.

KATE: I know you think I've been silly and frivolous, Dad –

WILLIAM: Occasionally ill-advised, certainly.

KATE: – but this time –

TOM makes violin-playing noises.

KATE: I've found him at last! The perfect man!

JANE: On the window sill?

WILLIAM: *(Trying to keep up spirits.)* Solomon doesn't think we should want things perfect. He thinks we should be busily seeking with a continual change. Like in the poem.

TOM: What poem?

SOLOMON: Sir Thomas Wyatt. The Lover Sheweth How He Is Forsaken of Such As He Sometime Enjoyed.

JANE: Have you asked Olinka to help you find it?

WILLIAM: Who?

JANE: *(Covering phone.)* Au pair. Ukrainian. Hardly speaks a word of –

(To SUSIE.) I'm sorry, but you know what Daddy said. You're responsible for your own tack.

KATE: Well – my busy seeking is finally over.

JANE: Susie, I'm at Gramps.

KATE: We were both in the bar at the Wolseley, waiting for people who were late. And I knew him at once, and he knew me and –

JANE: Of course I don't hate you. But I'm a hundred miles away and –

WILLIAM: *(To JANE.)* Oh, for heaven's sake – Give that here.

He wants an excuse to hide his confusion.

JANE: *(To WILLIAM.)* She can't find the saddle soap.

WILLIAM: Susie – get Olinka to take you to the saddler's in Banbury –

JANE: Olinka can't drive.

TOM: I'm very happy for you.

KATE: Thanks.

She hugs him.

JANE: And she's afraid of horses.

WILLIAM: But Ukrainians are Cossacks, aren't they?

SOLOMON: They won't know about saddle soap, though, they ride bareback.

WILLIAM: Oh, God – Wait a minute, Susie, wait a minute –

(To JANE.) Who lives near you who might have some?

JANE: Marilyn. Marilyn Connolly.

WILLIAM: *(To SUSIE.)* When Daddy comes home, get him to take you over to Marilyn's and borrow hers.

KATE: You'll like him. You really will. He loves diving.

TOM: *(Dirty.)* Oooh!

She giggles.

WILLIAM: Of course she will, if you ask nicely. What time does the gymkhana start?

KATE: We're going to have four children.

TOM: Hugo won't approve of that.

KATE: Oh, Hugo!

WILLIAM: Then you'll have all morning to make your saddle shine like your lovely little nose. And here's a little secret for you. No one will see whether your saddle's been polished or not so long as you don't fall off. So stay on! All right? Good luck. Bye, Susie.

Switches off.

TOM: You know, Dad, I think we do need champagne. It's not just Kate we have to celebrate –

WILLIAM: *(Alarmed.)* You're not engaged too?

TOM: Not exactly. But I am a father.

(Very proud.) Got a little boy. Three months old.

KATE: Three months! And you've waited all this time to tell us?

JANE: *(Unable to hide the jealousy.)* You would go and have a boy!

TOM: *(To WILLIAM.)* He's called William, after you.

WILLIAM: I'm flattered.

SOLOMON: May we know who his mother is?

TOM: *(Careful.)* I call her Polly.

JANE: Polly?

TOM: Short for Polynesian. It's easier than her real name.

JANE: Well!

Everyone else except SOLOMON is silenced.

SOLOMON: Congratulations!

TOM: Thanks.

The silence lasts a moment, then the front door opens and HUGO comes in. He is a year younger than KATE, dressed for cycling and out of breath. He has a large plaster on his head and is carrying several recyclable shopping bags. KATE runs over and kisses him.

KATE: Hi, darling! I'm engaged!

HUGO: To anyone you know?

She slaps him playfully.

HUGO: Hi, Dad.

WILLIAM: Will you please not all keep saying Hi!

HUGO: Happy birthday.

(Showing bag.) Brought you some samphire.

WILLIAM: How very kind.

> *(Relieved by change of subject.)* But you seem to have had a fearful time gathering it. Did you fall halfway down the cliff?

HUGO: What?

WILLIAM: The plaster.

HUGO: Oh, the police were trying to kettle us, and we weren't having that, so –

> *(Shrug.)* Standard operating procedure. Beat the shit out of the nearest protester.

SOLOMON: Oh, you were at the climate camp.

TOM: What's a climate camp?

HUGO: A place where responsible people get together to do something about the future of the planet.

KATE: *(Kissing him again.)* Oh, good, you brought your soapbox.

WILLIAM: What's this?

JANE: Troublemakers.

SOLOMON: It was on the news last night. After you'd gone to bed. They're planning to build a new coal-fired power station near Swansea.

HUGO: Can you believe it? Coal-fired! When the earth is choking to death from carbon dioxide!

JANE: Bernard says –

HUGO: There's a picture in the *Guardian.* Didn't you see it?

SOLOMON: We don't take a daily paper any more. Bad for your dad's blood pressure.

HUGO: Me being bashed by a policeman. Not wearing a number, of course. I've got it here.

He starts looking in one of his bags.

JANE: I'm sure he was only doing his duty.

HUGO: *(Genuine anger.)* If it's his duty to beat and batter and not infrequently kill people who are trying to tell the truth, yes. If not –

Awkward silence. He produces the paper and shows it to WILLIAM, who frowns over it.

HUGO: That's the back of my head. There.

WILLIAM looks from the picture to HUGO and back again.

WILLIAM: Hmm.

He hands the paper to SOLOMON, who looks at it, then at HUGO.

SOLOMON: *(Doubtful.)* I *think* it's him.

HUGO: *(Cross.)* Of course it is.

SOLOMON hands the paper to KATE.

KATE: *(Loyal to HUGO.)* Yes, look at the ears.

She passes the paper to TOM, and puts her arm round HUGO.

KATE: Poor you!

TOM: Quite a crack he gave you.

HUGO: Certainly was.

TOM: *(Handing paper to JANE.)* Look at that.

JANE: *(Refusing it.)* My sympathy's entirely with the police. They've got so much to do already, with all these rioters and so on, without you people –

HUGO: *(Stifling his anger.)* You don't change, do you?

JANE: No. I've always thought change very overrated.

TOM gives the paper back to HUGO.

KATE: Tell him about your baby, Tom.

TOM: You remember Polly? When you came to see me last year? We've had a boy.

HUGO: *(Beat.)* I thought we agreed, given world overpopulation –

TOM: You agreed, perhaps! You and Chloe!

KATE: How is Chloe?

HUGO: She – We've agreed to go our different ways.

JANE: Good!

HUGO: It's perfectly friendly. I admire her very much – she knows a huge amount about ecology. But she – she doesn't really like discussing things, she –

JANE: Likes pontificating! Like you!

HUGO: I don't pontificate! I look at the facts. I *think* about them. Then I say what I think.

JANE: You pontificate.

HUGO: If you ever stopped to think for one second, you might –

SOLOMON intervenes, looking in HUGO's bag.

SOLOMON: This isn't samphire. It's glasswort.

HUGO: Marsh samphire.

SOLOMON: Hmm.

HUGO: *(Annoyed.)* It's just as good. Some people think better.

SOLOMON: Mmm.

HUGO: You have to soak it, then –

SOLOMON: Don't teach your grandmother to suck eggs.

HUGO: I don't eat eggs.

SOLOMON: So you *are* vegan.

HUGO: You blanch it, then –

SOLOMON: I know.

HUGO: *(Handing him another bag.)* I don't want to be a nuisance, but –

JANE laughs unkindly.

HUGO: *(Ignoring her.)* After the samphire, if I could have a baked potato, with mushroom filling.

JANE: Please.

HUGO: I'll prepare it myself, of course.

SOLOMON: You most certainly will not! I'm cook in this house. And I've got you a cauliflower.

HUGO: Organic?

SOLOMON takes the bag with a sniff of contempt for such a silly question.

KATE: I thought they'd decided organic was no better for you than the other.

HUGO: *(Satirical.)* Oh, yes, and there's no eco-collapse coming so we can all go on drilling oil wells till kingdom come.

KATE: There's a nice logical leap!

HUGO: Everything's connected, if you'll only think about it.

JANE: Like you being so pasty is with being vegan.

WILLIAM: Solomon, are we having this champagne or not?

SOLOMON: Coming right up.

SOLOMON goes.

KATE: *(To HUGO.)* You know, you ought to go about with your own cook and taster. Like a medieval monarch.

WILLIAM: Or Pol Pot. For whom you seem to be in training.

KATE: Tell us about Polly, Tom.

TOM: She's eighteen.

JANE: *(Shocked.)* Eighteen!

TOM: Girls in the islands mature much earlier than here.

WILLIAM: They age earlier, too, don't they?

KATE: But that's nice. She and Tom can grow old together.

JANE: Well, I think –

KATE: Careful. Thinking can lead to wrinkling. Lines round
the eyes. Best not to risk it.

(To TOM.) I suppose William'll be too young to be a page at
my wedding?

TOM: I'm afraid so.

KATE: And Polly can't really be a bridesmaid if she's got a
baby. But you will bring them both?

TOM: Thank you.

WILLIAM: What colour is my namesake?

TOM: Golden brown.

KATE: Like Hovis?

TOM: I could certainly eat him. He smells – just heavenly.

JANE: *(Inspite of herself.)* Ah!

HUGO: But – Can't you see? It's simply immoral to bring
another child into a world where there are far too many
people already.

JANE: Then why don't you go and jump off a cliff. That'll even
things up.

WILLIAM: Children –

KATE: Milo and I are going to have two boys, two girls, and
two gays.

HUGO: That's just silly.

KATE: Hugo – darling – it was a joke.

HUGO: *(Passionate.)* It's far too serious to joke about. Can't you see? The world supply of basic commodities is going to –

WILLIAM: Please! This is a birthday party, not a political rally.

HUGO: *(Pained and angry.)* Oh, yes, ignore me, ignore anything I have to say! You always have done!

KATE: Darling –

HUGO: The only person in this family who ever listened to me was Mum!

WILLIAM: She did tend to spoil you, yes.

JANE is about to say something, but TOM puts a finger to his lips and she refrains.

HUGO: *(Deliberately aggressive.)* Solomon's still here, then?

WILLIAM: What?

HUGO: Mum died two years ago. And he's a psychiatric nurse and there's a terrible shortage.

WILLIAM: You mean, I'm not yet mad enough to need one?

HUGO: All you need is someone to help you in and out of your chair. And quite soon you won't need even that, will you?

WILLIAM: I'll be dead, you mean?

HUGO: Besides which, a white man having a black one to look after him – it's just not acceptable.

WILLIAM: *(Furious.)* Is it not.

Uncomfortable silence.

JANE: Actually, Daddy, Bernard and I were talking about this place. It was perfect for Mummy, of course. The noise in London – the fire engines, the ambulances – the aeroplanes! But here – peace, perfect peace.

KATE: Jane, that's what people put on gravestones.

JANE: Bernard and I were thinking, your memories here must be very sad.

WILLIAM: Not at all. Val had no idea what was going on, but she was quite happy. Enviable, really.

JANE: Well, but when you move –

WILLIAM: Not going anywhere in this chair.

JANE: You're not going to be in that for ever.

(Nanny.) You have to keep working at getting better, you know. It doesn't just happen. Bernard and I were thinking –

KATE: Again! You're living very dangerously, Jane.

JANE: *(Ignoring her.)* Suppose you get ill again. It's so far from where any of us live.

WILLIAM: I have Solomon. So long as Hugo will let me.

HUGO sets his face.

JANE: Bernard and I would like you to come and live with us. The house is so big – we could make you your own flat, with your own front door – You wouldn't be on your own, like you are here.

WILLIAM: *(Furious again.)* I see. Get rid of Solomon, and be beholden to you. How kind.

JANE: We're only thinking –

KATE: Again! I really think you should consult your beautician.

WILLIAM: *(Relieved to have something to talk about.)* I've never had a proper home, you know. Not till here. Not since Stratford. Which I didn't, as you may have gathered, much care for. Though it did give me the secret of my success. Such as it is.

KATE: No fishing!

JANE: If you're going to tell us again about Grandpa's shop –

WILLIAM: I've thought about it a lot since I was ill. Me peering over the counter, looking at the tourists, amazed at how keen they were to buy what I could see, even at five and six, was the most terrible tat. Watching them troop reverently into Anne Hathaway's cottage. Though Dad told us his grandfather built most of it himself. I was very puzzled. Why were they so excited? And then, when I was thirteen or so – It suddenly dawned on me. The pilgrims – it didn't matter whether or not they understood Shakespeare – who, after all, understands God? – they came to feel in touch with something larger than themselves. There were only a few holy sights in Stratford, but some people, the ones who bought the larger, more expensive busts of Old Bill, or the collected plays, they wanted to believe they saw more profoundly into them than other people. That they had a deeper insight into the genius of the place. And then – the nearest to inspiration I've ever had – I realized the more exclusive you made their way of seeing these things, the more they'd pay and the happier they'd be.

HUGO: Intellectual snobs.

WILLIAM: Yes! Always a very rich niche market. Let people persuade themselves they're travellers in the realms of gold, getting true secrets of goodly states and kingdoms which other people are missing. Sell them something intangible. But the result of that inspiration, if that's what it was –

KATE: I said, no fishing!

WILLIAM: – is I've spent my life on the move. In hotels, rented apartments, flats. Your mother and I gave you all a home in London, but – you're right, Jane – I was hardly ever there.

It was Valerie's home, your home, not mine. But this is mine. And though it's nice to know you all want me on my feet again, if only to walk away from it, I don't want to go. Sorry.

Silence.

KATE: Good for you.

WILLIAM: Thank you.

HUGO: The carbon footprint must be enormous. All this glass.

TOM: For heaven's sake –

HUGO: *(Carefully restrained.)* Oil is running out. In twenty or thirty years it will all have gone. Leaving an ecological wasteland behind it. And this place probably without any form of heating.

WILLIAM: I shall be dead in twenty years, even if I survive this afternoon.

HUGO: That's just – that's just typical of the way people shrug their way out of facing the facts. Oh, it's all beyond me, there's nothing one person can do. So I'll just turn the thermostat up a couple of degrees and read a nice book till we end with a bang not a whimper.

JANE: Bernard says, we don't really have to worry. The world has its own way of righting itself. And someone will find a way of helping it. Someone always has done in the past.

HUGO: This isn't like anything in the past.

TOM: But what *can* one person do?

HUGO: A lot. Look what's happened to rubbish, for instance.

JANE laughs scornfully.

HUGO: You sort your rubbish into different bags, don't you? What can and what can't be recycled?

JANE: Well, Mrs Hackett does, yes, she understands these
things, but –

HUGO: A few years ago no one recycled anything. It all
rotted away – or didn't – in toxic landfill. But a few people
saw how stupid that was. They started a movement. The
movement grew. Now – Every important change comes
about from a few individuals seeing the truth, pointing it
out, and going on pointing it out, till other people see it
too. That's how we change things. Starting small, then –

WILLIAM: Oh, it's a revival.

HUGO: What?

WILLIAM: We had small is beautiful in the Sixties. Charming
while it lasted.

HUGO: Is it really so clever to be ironic about the future of the
human race?

Silence.

We have to find alternative sources of energy – rediscover
old ways of living –

WILLIAM: May I ask – just for information – while you're
saving the world – what happens to the Wild Life
department of the company which I put you in charge of?

HUGO: We close it.

KATE: Steady. That's a very healthy profit you're making.

HUGO: I'm resigning. And I don't mean we should close just
the Wild Life department, I mean the whole company.

JANE: For heaven's sake –

HUGO: Encouraging people to fly from one continent to
another in pursuit of their own pleasure and our profit,
we're simply climate change criminals.

KATE: But we set aside a lot of money each year to plant trees
to offset –

HUGO: It's not just the CO_2.

KATE: Then what else?

HUGO: *(To WILLIAM.)* I was very happy when you put me in charge of the department, Dad. So many animals were being threatened. I thought tourism could bring positive benefits.

TOM: And so it does.

HUGO: Some, yes. Short-term ones. But –

(To KATE.) You took a stingray tour to the Cayman Islands. Tell them what it was like.

KATE: Wonderful. You can feed the rays, stroke them, swim with them –

HUGO: And help to exterminate them.

TOM: By swimming with them? Come on!

HUGO: By treating them as entertainment. We feed them squid to get them to come to our boats, but squid is not part of their usual diet. Now they're coming to rely on it. They're starting to lose the ability to look after themselves. Their immune systems are weakening. We've lured them out of their world and into ours, where they don't belong, any more than we belong in theirs. We're killing them.

TOM: Feed them something else.

HUGO: As for coral – Unless someone can find a way of removing the CO_2 which we've been dumping in the sea for two hundred years, all coral on the planet will be dead by 2050.

TOM: No. There are scientists working on –

HUGO: You're just denying the truth so you can go on doing what you like. Swimming with dolphins –

JANE: Oh, don't say that's bad too! Susie held a great big dolphin in her arms, she adored it!

HUGO: The dolphin probably enjoyed it too. Once they're used to us, dolphins like us very much. They start banging themselves against the keels of boats to get our attention. They damage themselves on the propellers. They enjoy being with us so much they can't be bothered to look after their young. They abandon them.

KATE: Is *that* true?

HUGO: Yes. Wherever man goes, he destroys.

Silence.

WILLIAM: So I've spent my life destroying the planet. Is that what you're saying?

HUGO: You weren't to know when you started. But now, when you do know, it must be wicked to continue, mustn't it?

WILLIAM: Thus the rude son strikes his father dead.

TOM: What?

KATE: Shakespeare. Bound to be.

HUGO: When the oceans rise, deltas everywhere – the Amazon, the Ganges, the Yangtze – even the Thames, in its small way – What do you think the people who live in those crowded places are going to do? They're going to force their way to higher ground. Where there are too many people already. And those too many are going to resist them. There's going to be war. Everywhere.

WILLIAM: That's too despairing, Hugo.

HUGO: The history of the world is the history of population movements, Dad. Fighting for land. People are pouring out of Asia already, as they poured out in the Dark Ages. And – you don't read the papers.

WILLIAM: No.

HUGO: Every day another rickety boat sinks in the Mediterranean, drowning more Africans desperate to escape their hopeless lives. There's going to be more and more of them. And every country with an atom or a hydrogen bomb will use it to try and stop them. The human race – well! Imagine it.

SOLOMON returns with champagne and glasses. KATE sees him.

KATE: Only just in time, Solomon. Hugo was about to wipe out the entire human race.

SOLOMON: Sorry to be so long.

WILLIAM: Very eloquent, Hugo. Very powerful. And not inapposite to what I'm going to say.

(To them all.) I've asked you here not just to celebrate my birthday, and my survival from the operation, but to discuss the future of the company as well. Which is why I now give you three pieces of information, which may alter your thinking, though probably not Hugo's, he's so clear about everything already.

HUGO: I believe everything I've said.

WILLIAM: Nothing more blinding than faith. Now – the first piece of information is – knowing of my illness, another company wants to buy us. It's a serious offer. Even a generous one, given the current economic situation. Number two, even if we don't sell, I'm giving up being Chief Executive Officer. Doctor's orders.

(Indicates pillbox.) Stress and all that. I shall stay on as chairman, if we decide not to sell, but a new CEO will be needed. The third item is that at eleven o'clock this morning Solomon and I became civil partners.

WILLIAM waves a certificate to prove it. Complete silence. Then SOLOMON pops open the champagne.

WILLIAM: Perhaps you'd like to drink to our happiness.

Freeze.

Blackout.

Act two

The garden. Later that afternoon.

JANE, TOM and KATE are in different areas of the garden, on their mobiles. HUGO is on a bench, turning the pages of the 'Guardian', while listening to the others.

KATE is talking to MILO.

KATE: It's pretty amazing. A cocky middle-aged skeleton waltzing out of the family closet, grinning its gay head off!

TOM is talking to his business adviser.

TOM: So children don't have automatic inheritance rights, but spouses do?

JANE is talking to BERNARD.

JANE: He showed us a certificate thing. Waved it about. What the government thought it was doing –

HUGO: *(Not looking up.)* Good. It thought it was doing good. Which it was.

JANE glares at him

KATE: No, proper African. Black. With that lovely purplish bloom, you know?

TOM: 49 per cent is held in a trust. For us children.

JANE: Oh, don't worry about Susie, she can look after herself for a change. Though how we're going to explain it to the twins –

HUGO: If I were you, I'd let them explain it to you.

She glares at him again.

KATE: I'm rather knocked sideways, actually. I always got on so much better with him than with Mum. I thought we were – you know – we had a special relationship.

TOM: It's being tax efficient in Lichtenstein or somewhere. He controls it. Like everything else.

JANE: Couldn't we challenge it in the courts? Unsound mind or something?

KATE: Of course I can't ask. Could you ask your father?

She laughs. JANE glances over.

TOM: So what do you reckon a generous bid might be? In the current climate?

HUGO looks up.

JANE: She's not taking it seriously, of course. She's got engaged again.

HUGO: *(To TOM.)* How much does he say?

TOM waves him away impatiently.

JANE: Oh, some brewer.

KATE: At least it explains why he was hardly ever at home.

JANE: Well, I'm not sure. He was fine to begin with. But then he suddenly came out with this. What's so funny about that? Oh, 'come out'. Really, Bernard –

TOM: All right. Thanks a lot, Jack. Really helpful.

KATE: God knows what other surprises he has in store for us.

JANE: I think perhaps he's ashamed. I certainly hope so. Bye.

KATE: Bye, darling.

She makes brief kissing noises. JANE, TOM and KATE come together. HUGO stays where he is.

JANE: Bernard's having to stay late at the office again. It's two or three nights a week now.

HUGO: *(Flat.)* Poor Bernard.

JANE's mobile goes. She looks at it.

KATE: Susie?

JANE: I'm not answering.

(Putting phone away.) I can't be always looking after her.

HUGO: No. Much better send her away to school.

KATE: Yes, let professionals deal with her.

JANE: It's for her own good.

KATE: Of course!

TOM: All right, enough bickering, let's –

JANE: I'm not bickering. I don't bicker. They do.

KATE laughs.

JANE: If you'd stop giggling for a moment –

KATE: But you're so funny!

JANE: Bernard wants to know – Did any of you have any idea about – about Daddy?

KATE: Not a sausage!

TOM: I have wondered about Solomon. But I thought he probably went to Hereford on his day off and –

KATE: Hereford?

HUGO: *(Not looking up.)* It's full of SAS men.

KATE: *(Pretending interest.)* Oh?

JANE: *(Glare.)* The point is – Has anyone any idea how long it's been going on?

TOM: Not me.

KATE: What difference would it make?

JANE: Well, if it's to do with Daddy being ill, you see –

HUGO: He had a problem with his aorta, not his sexuality.

JANE: If you want to join this conversation, Hugo, will you please join it properly!

HUGO: *(Not moving.)* Homosexuality's not an illness.

JANE: I'm not so sure about that.

HUGO: You mean, Bernard hasn't told you what to think about it yet?

TOM: Please –

JANE: Anyway, it may not be a physical thing.

KATE: Come on!

JANE: What Bernard means is, Solomon may have been using undue influence to persuade Daddy while he wasn't feeling himself.

KATE: So he felt him instead?

TOM: Kate –

JANE: If Daddy had ever been – that way inclined – before – Mummy wouldn't have stood for it. Not for a second.

KATE: Perhaps she never found out.

JANE: Perhaps she did, and was so upset, that's why she lost her mind.

HUGO: Oh, Jane!

TOM: Yes, I don't think –

JANE: It might have tipped the balance.

KATE: If Mum had known and felt bad about it, she'd have got a divorce. Double quick.

TOM: Yes. She didn't muck about. Now shall we –

JANE: But she may have been thinking of us. How bad divorce is for the children. Mummy always put us before herself.

HUGO: *(Rising now.)* Really? I remember a series of barely English-speaking au pairs while she went off to work.

JANE: *(Unhappy.)* She wanted to play her full part in the business, of course.

KATE: At least she didn't pack us off to boarding schools.

TOM: Kate –

KATE: And perhaps she did know about Dad and didn't mind.

JANE: Of course she'd have minded!

KATE: Perhaps she thought him getting his rocks off with other men was better than him getting them off with other women.

JANE: Don't be so disgusting! Poor Mummy!

TOM: All right, all right. Now, since Hugo has kindly consented to join us, can we discuss this offer for the company?

KATE: Alleged offer.

TOM: What do you mean?

KATE: It may be one of Dad's tests. We've all lived off the company all our lives. Maybe he wants to see how much we actually care about it. And him.

JANE: *(Careful.)* We're very proud of what he's created, of course.

HUGO: Speak for yourself.

TOM: You weren't ashamed to work for him.

HUGO: I didn't then know what I do now.

TOM: Then do you not want to be part of the discussion?

HUGO: Oh, yes. You'll all outvote me, of course, so you can go on making money, but –

TOM: I certainly hope so.

HUGO: But as I'm going to devote my life from now on to –

JANE: *(Sneer.)* Saving the world?

HUGO: *(Ignoring this.)* You're none of you going to agree to close the company, are you?

JANE: No.

TOM: No.

KATE: What would be the point? As soon as we shut up shop, other companies would move in and snaffle up our business.

HUGO: Our consciences would be clear.

JANE: My conscience *is* clear. I'm thinking of my children.

HUGO: All right, then. I'll vote to sell. But no one's going to buy it with Dad still controlling forty-nine per cent through Mum's trust.

TOM: Suppose not.

HUGO: So before any sale, he'll have to dissolve it. And divvy up the cash. Which is what you all want, isn't it?

JANE: You know, Hugo, sometimes you talk real sense.

KATE: *(To HUGO.)* Not worried that your share might be just a little tainted?

HUGO: I can untaint it again by how I use it. What will you spend yours on? Parties?

KATE: One huge End of the World party! Coming?

TOM: Jack thinks the company's worth about seventy million, which means –

KATE: Not with turnover so badly down.

TOM: No?

KATE: We've suffered less than sub-prime Sun and Sangria. But we've still suffered. Sixty million's more like it.

Beat.

JANE: Forty-nine per cent of sixty is –

HUGO: We'd each get about seven and a half million.

The others look at him in surprise.

KATE: *(To TOM.)* Enough for you?

TOM: More than enough. It would save my life.

HUGO: Hurray! Now you can go and kill more coral.

JANE: *(Wondering.)* Seven and a half *million*. And we can spend it how we like?

HUGO: Yes, you can pay off the mortgage on that ridiculously large house you bought at the top of the market.

JANE: It was for the children! So they wouldn't have to grow up in London, with all the dirt and crime and –

KATE: Blacks.

JANE: Bernard said –

HUGO: Bonkers Bernard the batty banker! Talk about negative equity!

TOM: Enough! Let's have a formal vote for selling.

He and JANE and HUGO raise their hands.

TOM: Kate?

KATE hesitates.

JANE: Come on, Kate.

KATE: I don't need money. Milo has squillions. But I want to have a big family, so I want to give up work. So everything inclines me to say, Sell. But – Not sure.

TOM: Dad won't pay any attention if we're divided.

KATE: It's him I'm worried about. It's been his life.

JANE: I think we've considered him too much. Let's consider ourselves for a change.

HUGO: *(Laughing.)* For a change, Jane?

KATE: I need time to think about it. So – if you'll excuse me, I'll go for a ponder in the rose garden.

TOM: Not too long a one, please.

JANE's mobile goes and she answers it without thinking.

JANE: Hello? Oh, Susie.

(To others.) Damn!

(To SUSIE.) No, he's got to stay late at the office. Didn't he ring you?

KATE goes.

JANE: Well, you'll just have to wait till tomorrow morning. I'm sorry, but it's entirely your own fault, and there's nothing I can do. So I suggest you go to bed early and get a good night's sleep. Goodbye.

Switches off.

I need to get away from this place. It's spoiled for me now.

TOM: Want to walk to the village?

JANE: Good idea. I need to clear my head, after all I've learned this afternoon.

(Anxious.) It's not going to rain, is it?

HUGO: Fat chance. There's been a drought for the last six months.

JANE: All right, Tom. Let's go, before he starts up again.

They start to go.

HUGO: *(Calling after them.)* There'll be a lot of blood spilt over water when the world's supply starts running out.

JANE: *(Off.)* Most of it yours, with luck.

HUGO leafs through the paper, then looks up to see SOLOMON coming from the house with a small first aid box. Without the others present, HUGO is anxious to make a better impression.

HUGO: Hi! What have you got there?

SOLOMON: Time to change that dressing.

HUGO: It's OK.

SOLOMON: No, it's not. It's filthy. You just sit still for five minutes while I –

HUGO does what he's told. During the following scene SOLOMON removes the old plaster and applies a new dressing.

HUGO: Sorry I came on a bit strong before.

SOLOMON: Did you?

HUGO: Being vegan – it's a matter of principle. Our relation to nature. To the animal kingdom.

SOLOMON: What about the vegetable kingdom?

HUGO: What about it?

SOLOMON: What about carrots, for instance? Do you think they like being hauled out of the ground by their hair?

HUGO: Oh, but –

SOLOMON: Do cauliflowers cheer when they see you coming down the garden with a knife in your hand?

HUGO: Carrots and cauliflowers don't have cerebral cortices. They don't feel pain.

SOLOMON: Sit still! They bleed when you cut them, don't they?

HUGO: Not actual blood.

SOLOMON: *(Beat.)* How much do you believe of what you say, Hugo? How much is just to annoy?

HUGO: I have to annoy sometimes. I mean, Jane, she's really –

SOLOMON laughs.

HUGO: Tom's just as bad. He never listens to me. Never has done. Kate does. Sometimes. As for Dad –

SOLOMON: I listen. And what I hear is you making as much trouble as possible – for me, for William, for anyone else who happens to be around. You've upset William very much. All this about closing the company.

HUGO: It would make people sit up and think. Shock tactics are sometimes the only –

SOLOMON: William created the company from nothing. He and your Mum. He's given it his whole life.

HUGO: I know, but –

SOLOMON: And he's given you a very good education on the profits. Every opportunity to go off and make a career of your own, like Tom's tried to. But no, you've preferred to stay and draw a very nice salary, much bigger than you'd've got anywhere else, you've wafted round the world watching whales and stingrays and lions and tigers, and then you turn round, when you've seen them all, and he's been ill and nearly died, and you denounce him as a criminal. That's not very grateful, is it?

HUGO: I didn't say he was a criminal –

SOLOMON: Yes, you did. A climate change criminal.

HUGO: It was – Perhaps I shouldn't have put it so strongly,
    but –

SOLOMON: You put everything too strongly. Always.

HUGO: Well, I get that from him.

SOLOMON works on him a moment.

SOLOMON: Do you want us out of here?

HUGO: No, not at all.

SOLOMON: Sounded like it to us. Tom and Jane, they're open
    about what they want. Kate – she thinks about William
    and what he might want. But you – you talk such grand
    generalities. What you really want, and why, we've no
    idea.

HUGO: I want to make people aware of the facts. They're
    easy enough to find, they're in the papers, the TV, but
    people simply won't face them. They skip them or switch
    channels. And politicians – they don't get elected by telling
    the truth, not when it means asking people to change the
    way we all live.

SOLOMON nods.

HUGO: That's why we have to start politics all over again,
    from the bottom. In local communities. Individuals
    getting together, forming small units, the units joining
    together, creating larger communities, explaining the
    dangers of continued unrestricted growth, working for the
    fundamental changes which –

SOLOMON: That's what I mean. All very grand and general.
    It may be true, but what are you actually doing about it
    yourself?

HUGO: Some colleagues and I are going to set up a network
    to keep communities in touch with each other. An open
    forum, you might say. A serious parliament, not a squabble
    of short-term self-seekers like we have now.

SOLOMON: And where are you going to do that?

HUGO: It'll be online. But we'll need a base, and as a matter of fact I was thinking of asking –

SOLOMON: *(Alarmed.)* Here? You want to move in here?

HUGO: If you could let us have the small barn – We'd do it up ourselves. We wouldn't disturb you. And we'd look after this place when you went to London. Be on hand if anything –

SOLOMON: So what you're offering is – instead of us moving in with Jane, you and your mates move in with us.

HUGO: I'm afraid Jane just wants Dad.

SOLOMON: Tell me about it.

(Beat.) So you're not upset about William and me?

HUGO: Surprised. But I've never felt I knew Dad. Or he me. He patted me on the head now and then, but – Families!

SOLOMON finishes bandaging.

SOLOMON: There!

HUGO: Thanks.

SOLOMON: I've had three, you know. Families. The first was killed by the rebels. I survived by hiding between my mother's body and the wall of our hut. When I crept out, thinking they'd gone, the commander decided it was funnier to make me a soldier than to shoot me. Gave me a sort of uniform. And a gun. Made me his mascot. For three years we moved about, never stopping anywhere for more than a few days, living off the land. Not much opportunity to be vegan.

HUGO is silent.

SOLOMON: You talk about the world's got to do this, the world's got to do that. But only very privileged people can make choices. About what they eat, what they wear, where they live. The rest of us live as best we can.

HUGO: I do understand that. All the same –

SOLOMON: I never thought of shooting the commander, though I had plenty of opportunity. I'd become one of them, you see. My second family. But then things went wrong and we fell into an ambush and – I survived by running away faster than anyone else. Then the missionaries found me and sent me to England, and the couple who adopted me, the Birlinghams, they were very kind, very decent. Selfless, but single-minded. Sent me to a boarding school with the notion I'd go back to Africa as a missionary myself. But then – Oh, my God, we've done all this for him and he turns out to be one of those!

HUGO: Yes, African bishops aren't very good about –

SOLOMON: I was like a swallow with a broken wing. I'd flown all the way across the Sahara to England, but couldn't fly back. I'd had three families and lost all of them. What could I do now? I could be a nurse. Going here and there, sharing other people's homes for a while, becoming 'one of the family', but never for long, and never having one of my own. Always truly homeless. And homesick. Not for Africa. God, no! For somewhere I only dreamed of. You can go a long way on dreams. A long time. But now I've found it. I'm home.

(Beat.) But I'm not sure I can share it with you.

During this speech, WILLIAM has wheeled himself on inside the house. He listens to the end of the scene.

HUGO: Why not?

SOLOMON: You're too abrasive. Too like William. I think you'd kill him. He does so enjoy a row. He's in a terrible bait with Evan Prichard at the moment, because of the spring.

77

HUGO: Oh.

SOLOMON: It's very bad for his blood pressure. And Mr Prichard, though he was kind to your Mum, he's always been suspicious of me because I'm African, and his aunty had an affair with a black American soldier in the war, and a baby and –

HUGO: I never knew that.

SOLOMON: Nor did I till last week, when I met his daughter in Waitrose and she explained. It was only sixty-five years ago, you see, his aunty being naughty in Newport. Still fresh in the memory.

HUGO laughs.

SOLOMON: So would you do something for me? Would you go and see him and ask him, very politely, how long he plans to keep the pump going. Explain how it upsets William and the pump in his heart. Suggest we come to some agreement about how and when pumps should be used.

HUGO: All right.

SOLOMON: Be tactful. Don't say he's got to stop raising bullocks this very evening because they fart so much CO_2 into the atmosphere. Deal with a real, cranky man in the real, cranky world. Then I might talk to William about you having the barn.

HUGO: Thank you.

SOLOMON: I admire your dream. Much less selfish than mine. But – you do have this habit of telling people how to do things. How to cook samphire, for instance.

HUGO: I'm sorry, I –

SOLOMON: It's OK. Just be tactful with Prichard.

(Rising.) I must get on. Seen Kate?

HUGO: She's pondering in the rose garden.

SOLOMON: Could you tell her William wants to talk to her?

HUGO: Of course.

HUGO goes. After a moment WILLIAM wheels himself out.

WILLIAM: Is it safe? He has gone?

SOLOMON: He's all right. Talks a lot of sense. It's only the way he talks it is so annoying.

WILLIAM: Quite a test you've set him.

SOLOMON: We'll see.

WILLIAM: *(Restless.)* I can't bear it that he says we can't go and see birds and animals any more. We live in such a ghastly electronic hum – if we only know a virtual world, not the real one – If we lose touch with nature, we lose touch with our own nature, too.

(Beat.) I suppose that sounds like a tired old man.

SOLOMON: Not a good nap, then?

WILLIAM: Hardly closed my eyes. And when I did – Hugo's fault. I kept imagining I was high up in the sky, with the world below me, like a map. The blue sea was rising over the green land. It didn't stop at the estuaries, it came up and up, fiercer and fiercer, driving the rivers back – it wasn't a map any more, it was real land and water – the rivers flooding over their banks, sheep and cattle running for high ground, the waves foaming after them like – People were clinging to trees, losing hold, falling – There was one woman, she looked like Kate, she had a baby –

He stops.

WILLIAM: It was awful. Like being dead but at the same time alive in the future.

SOLOMON takes his hand.

SOLOMON: Want me to stay when Kate – ?

WILLIAM: No. Yes. I don't know.

SOLOMON: You've always got on better with her than the others.

WILLIAM: Makes it worse.

SOLOMON kisses him on the top of his head. They look at each other.

WILLIAM: I'll manage.

KATE is coming on.

WILLIAM: *(Falsely jolly.)* Hello!

KATE: Hi! Oh, sorry!

He laughs.

KATE: Jane's in an awful stew about you two, you know.

(To SOLOMON.) She thinks you bewitched him.

WILLIAM: How silly.

(To SOLOMON.) I bewitched you, didn't I?

SOLOMON: This place bewitched both of us.

WILLIAM: But you never guessed?

KATE: *(Calm but careful.)* No. No, I thought it was one of your tests at first. Your bad taste jokes. Then – I don't know. You can't tell gays any more, you've all become so normal.

WILLIAM: Fancy Solomon, do you?

KATE: *(To SOLOMON.)* Could do.

(To WILLIAM.) Why did you never tell me?

WILLIAM: *(Taken aback.)* About him?

KATE: About fancying men.

WILLIAM: Oh, I – it's a long story, I –

KATE: I'm not Jane. I thought we told each other everything.

WILLIAM: No one ever does quite that, you know.

KATE: I told you.

(To SOLOMON.) He was like God. The person from whom no secrets were hid.

WILLIAM: I'm not God. Nothing like.

KATE: *(Beat, then to SOLOMON again.)* Did Mum know?

SOLOMON: She didn't know anything that was going on anywhere the last five years.

WILLIAM: But she liked you very much. Knew you when she didn't know who I was.

SOLOMON: She was always pleased when you came down, though. She knew you loved her.

KATE: Did you?

WILLIAM: Yes.

KATE: Honestly?

WILLIAM: We had an agreement, you see, Val and I –

SOLOMON prepares to go.

SOLOMON: You OK?

WILLIAM: Yes.

SOLOMON: Sure?

WILLIAM: Yes.

SOLOMON: More tea, Kate?

KATE: Please.

He goes.

KATE: *(Brisk.)* The others want you to sell. Provided the offer is good enough.

81

WILLIAM: Oh –

KATE: *(Surprised.)* Isn't that what you wanted to talk about?

WILLIAM: No.

KATE: *(Anxious.)* You – you're not – You haven't been fibbing about how well you are?

WILLIAM: No. I'm all right. Will be.

(Careful; a prepared speech.) Your mother, you know, – you're very like her. She was always having tremendous affairs. Great romantic folderols. When I first met her, I mean. At language school.

KATE: Good for her.

WILLIAM: But I hadn't had an affair in my life. I was stuck in terrible late adolescent, provincial and sometimes suicidal gloom and guilt. As queers were supposed to be in those days.

KATE: God!

WILLIAM: We were rather pathetic, really. I was, anyway. Thought it was the way things were. But Val didn't. Told me not to be so silly, and – Well, after the course, she went off to Strasbourg to be a translator and had lots more folderols, while I – anything to get away from Stratford and my father's tat shop – I took a job with Thomas Cook's in London and still had none. But when I went to see her out there she'd decided to find me someone. He was called Jean Karl. A dancer. Curly hair, sweet smile.

KATE: Your first?

WILLIAM: Afterwards, I didn't know what to say, so I said Merci beaucoup. And he corrected my pronunciation.

KATE laughs.

WILLIAM: The French, you know – natural schoolmasters. Well, after that my life, you could say, began. But Valerie had a problem. She wasn't – ordinary. She wanted independence, to have her own career and income – and all her lovers, she complained, wanted to provide and rule.

KATE: Witty!

WILLIAM: She was witty. But practical too. She decided she must live alone. I was romantic. I was looking for proper, permanent, life-long love. Marriage with another man, you could say, though you couldn't say it then.

KATE: This was when you were – ?

WILLIAM: Twenty-two, twenty-three. I was longing so badly to be settled – completed by my other half is how I thought of it – been reading Plato, as lonely young queers did in those days. Don't know what they read now.

KATE: They don't read at all. They watch porn on their computers.

WILLIAM: Still lonely, then. Well – while I kept looking in the wrong place, and finding the wrong person, I had a number of catastrophes. One of them tried to kill himself.

KATE: Oh, God.

WILLIAM: Valerie said it was just emotional blackmail, not a real attempt. But he nearly succeeded. And I was – not just heartbroken, because I'd loved him, or tried to – tried too hard, I expect – but desolate. I thought I was never going to be any good at love. Ever. And at just that time Val was back in London, bored with translating other people's jumbled speeches, and even more bored with complacent, demanding men, by one of whom she'd just got pregnant –

KATE: What?

WILLIAM: By mistake. Or so she swore. But you women – can you ever tell what your bodies are up to?

KATE: What did she do?

WILLIAM: Well – She wanted to keep it. So we sat up all one night, drinking wine and thrashing around the pros and cons – and around dawn, we agreed to get married, found a specialist travel company and forget our distresses together. We would give each other the security from which to conduct our affairs with unsuitable men. I could do what I wanted abroad, she could do what she liked at home while I was away, but when we were together – we would present as a proper couple.

KATE: But that means Jane's not –

WILLIAM: *(Careful.)* That night was the only time I ever got near to going to bed with Valerie.

KATE: *(Startled.)* What?

WILLIAM: We were never lovers.

KATE: Wait a minute, wait a minute –

WILLIAM: I've done my best to be father to you all, but – Jane's right. It probably wasn't a very good best.

KATE: But –

(Sudden suspicion.) This isn't one of your tests, is it?

WILLIAM: No.

KATE: So who was – is – our father?

WILLIAM: Jane and Tom had one. You and Hugo had another.

KATE: *(Dazed, but trying to be cool.)* Well, at least that explains why I've never felt Jane was much of a sister.

WILLIAM: Both were married men with legitimate children. Val preferred her lovers to be married. They wanted to be able to drop her at the first sign of trouble, so it was easier for her to drop them.

KATE: She never talked like that to me.

WILLIAM: She might have done, if she hadn't –

KATE: *(Still dazed.)* What a – I mean – Mum – Shit!

Silence.

WILLIAM: It wasn't that unusual a situation. Quite traditional, in fact, specially among the aristocracy.

KATE: *(Head whirling.)* My father was a lord?

WILLIAM: *(Laugh.)* No, no.

KATE: Then who was he?

WILLIAM: *(Careful again.)* Val wouldn't tell me.

KATE: Oh, for God's sake –

WILLIAM: She said it might make it awkward if we met at parties. He was in our social circle, you see.

KATE: *(Attempted joke.)* Not a marquis, but at least one of our class!

WILLIAM: All she would say was that his wife was pregnant at the same time as she was herself – with you – and had a son. I often wondered, watching you at school plays and so on, if one of the boys was your brother.

KATE suddenly begins to fear what's coming.

WILLIAM: She was worried that one of you might want to marry a sibling. Jane was all right, because her father was not Bernard's, and apart from Jane only had sons, so Tom was OK too. Who their father was I don't know and never will now. But as she was getting ill, she gave me this envelope, and made me swear not to open it until you or Hugo got engaged. You've been engaged so often, I opened it some years ago.

He hands her the envelope. She opens it with dread. She glances at the paper inside. Then at WILLIAM.

KATE: *(Groan.)* Oh – oh, Dad, Dad, what have you done?

WILLIAM: As soon as you said Milo, I –

KATE: Milo – Milo –

She screws up the paper and throws it at him.

KATE: Why didn't you tell me? Why did you never tell me?

WILLIAM: I thought – it seemed so unlikely, I –

KATE: You've just ruined my whole life!

She runs at him, flailing with her fists, so he has to catch her hands.

WILLIAM: Kate – sweetheart – Shh – shh –

KATE: *(Sobbing in his arms.)* What am I going to do? Whatever am I going to do?

WILLIAM: I don't know. I don't know.

She waits a moment then pushes him away, trying to seem her normal self.

KATE: Well! No wonder my love life has been so erratic! With a false father and a promiscuous mother, what chance did I ever have of a normal relationship?

WILLIAM: Every chance. Because we both loved all of you.

KATE: Oh, so lying to us about who we were was a way of loving us, was it ?

He shrugs.

KATE: *(Bitter.)* When we were children, about the only thing you ever punished us for was lying.

He is silent.

KATE: I looked up to you. You were my Dad and I was your Kate. But now –

WILLIAM: Nothing has changed.

KATE: Oh, yes it has! I don't know who I am. I don't know who you are. Except you're not my father any more.

WILLIAM: I am. And always will be.

She shakes her head.

WILLIAM: In character, in spirit, you take after me. We just don't happen to be blood relatives.

KATE: But Milo and I are! And because of you, I've been having an affair with my own brother!

WILLIAM: It was a thousand to one –

KATE: *(Bitter.)* All it needs is for you to have had an affair with his father, and we'd be a really cosy family, wouldn't we!

WILLIAM: Kate, sweetheart –

KATE: *(In real pain.)* What was he like?

WILLIAM: I don't really know. I only met him a few times, at parties and things.

(Hoping to ease the tension.) He was very handsome, actually. I quite –

She just looks at him. He is more serious.

WILLIAM: When he died, people were very shocked. They liked him so much. And he was so young.

KATE: *(Effort.)* Do I look like him?

WILLIAM: No, you look like Val.

KATE: Mum. Whom I never really knew at all.

(Bewildered at his calm about it.) And you think this doesn't change anything?

WILLIAM: I'm still your father, to all intents and purposes. I've loved you, brought you up –

KATE: And bloodlines, DNA, genes – none of those things mattered, so long as Mummy could have her affairs and Daddy his boyfriends?

WILLIAM: What matters most is parental love. Whoever gives it.

KATE: Sounds a bit pervy, parental love, when Daddy's not actually your Daddy.

WILLIAM: Sweetheart –

KATE: Don't keep calling me that!

WILLIAM: Kate –

KATE: You've been false to me from the day I was born. The day I was conceived. Big Daddy God, the fraudulent father, ruling over children that weren't his!

WILLIAM: But you were mine.

(Self-justifying.) And Val absolutely didn't want you to know you weren't. Unless –

KATE: So it's all her fault! Now she's dead and can't defend herself!

WILLIAM: She thought – no, all right, we both thought – you, all of you, you'd be ashamed. Of us, I mean. I mean, think what Jane would have said.

KATE: Oh, fuck Jane! No wonder Mum lost her mind – lying to us, lying to everyone –

She weeps. Beat.

WILLIAM: *(Tentative.)* I don't see why you shouldn't marry Milo.

KATE: *(Shocked.)* Are you mad?

WILLIAM: We're not in the Old Testament. He's only your half-brother.

KATE: That's just revolting! The very idea –

WILLIAM: Of course, you mustn't –

KATE: *(Savage.)* Oh, you mean, it's perfectly all right, brothers and sisters, only they mustn't have children, they might turn out to have two heads, and that would be so difficult to explain to the midwife. For God's sake, even in Stratford, people must have had better morals than that.

WILLIAM: I'm sorry. If I'd known how you were going to take it –

KATE: What would you have done? Say nothing? Let me marry him, and the more heads the children had the better?

WILLIAM: Don't be like that, don't –

KATE: How do you want me to be? Calm and collected, take it on the chin? Well, I'm not calm and I'm not collected. You've just ripped my heart out!

WILLIAM: What can I say? I –

KATE: Don't say anything.

(Beat, pulling herself together.) And don't tell the others.

WILLIAM: All right. But – Milo has a sister, doesn't he? If she and Hugo –

KATE: *(Distracted.)* She's married. Lives in Seattle.

(Choke.) We were going to ask her to come back for the wedding, but –

(Struggles a moment.) Was Mum never really in love?

WILLIAM: Well – she wasn't looking for the perfect man. She didn't think there was one. So she always kept something in reserve.

KATE: *(Cold.)* You must have kept a lot in reserve yourself. Or not looked very hard.

WILLIAM: What do you mean?

KATE: You never committed yourself, did you?

WILLIAM: Apart from my early disasters, no. Till Solomon.

KATE: *(Bitter.)* Been inconvenient, wouldn't it? Might have had to let people know.

WILLIAM: That's not fair.

KATE: Us, for instance.

He is silent.

KATE: What a useful excuse we've been all these years. Never to love someone properly.

WILLIAM can't answer. She looks at the view.

KATE: *(Tears.)* We were going to have four children.

WILLIAM: You can still have children.

KATE: Not his. Oh, and I've always been so mean about Jane and how she blathers on about the twins –

(Recovering a little.) She'd better not know any of this. She thinks Mum was a saint. There'd be terrible wailing and weeping and gnashing of teeth.

(Trying to smile.) So this is where the swinging Sixties got us.

WILLIAM: Seventies, actually.

SOLOMON comes on with tea. He sees how stricken KATE looks. He puts the tea down, and puts his arms round her. Silence as she leans against him. He gently rubs her back.

SOLOMON: Want something stronger?

She shakes her head. He continues to hold her.

SOLOMON: You're very like your Mum, you know.

KATE: *(Muffled.)* Why did she do this to me?

SOLOMON: Because she was who she was. She knew people wanted her to go against her own nature, to be and do the ordinary things. But she wouldn't. And she saved William from trying to go against his. She gave him the courage.

KATE: *(To WILLIAM.)* Is that true?

WILLIAM: *(Simple.)* Yes.

KATE: But who's going to give me courage now?

She buries herself in SOLOMON's arms again, as JANE appears. She very much dislikes what she sees.

JANE: *(Suspicious.)* What's going on here?

SOLOMON: Life. As we call it.

KATE moves away from SOLOMON.

JANE: If you've been discussing the future of the company without the rest of us, Kate –

WILLIAM: Would she do that?

JANE's expression suggests that absolutely yes, she would. WILLIAM wants to deflect her attention from KATE. He rolls his chair over towards JANE. KATE pretends to go and look at the view.

WILLIAM: Where's Tom?

JANE: He stopped to watch a cricket match. As cricket is the biggest single reason I'm glad I don't have boys –

WILLIAM: You took the opportunity to come and bend my ear about how I should sell the company and give you most of the money.

SOLOMON: William –

JANE: *(Angry.)* We don't want anything the others don't want.

WILLIAM: *(Taken aback.)* I'm sorry.

JANE: You're so unfair. You always pick on Bernard and me. We want to know where we stand, that's all. Is that so unreasonable?

WILLIAM: No – no.

JANE: So what's Kate been saying?

WILLIAM: We weren't talking about the company.

JANE: *(Suspicious again.)* Well, Bernard and I have been. And we think you should sell. What you do with your half of the money is up to you, of course. We only want our share of Mummy's trust.

> *(Unable to stop herself, but carefully not looking at SOLOMON.)* And I have to say I'm very glad she's dead, because I know she would have been absolutely horrified by what you've told us today.

WILLIAM: Would she?

JANE: Yes.

> *WILLIAM glances over at KATE, wondering how he should respond. But she's not listening.*

WILLIAM: *(Glad to be on safer territory.)* Well – if you say so. But if we sell – have you considered that new owners might not want you to carry on with your art and culture tours?

JANE: I wouldn't be all that sorry. I'd have more time for the girls.

WILLIAM: But you said you wanted more time for the business. That's why you want to send them away to school.

JANE: *(Flustered.)* Well, yes, but – Bernard needs someone to help him. The social side is so important – dinner parties – taking clients to the theatre and the opera – the new Garsington and so on – And I've had so much experience of dealing with difficult people. The Rembrandt tour last January nearly killed me.

SOLOMON: The one for the Russian oligarch?

> *JANE avoids speaking to him direct.*

JANE: There were only five on it –

WILLIAM: But paying through the nose, as I remember.

JANE: Mr Gargarov didn't care what it cost. He's got what he thinks is a Rembrandt self-portrait on one of his yachts.

SOLOMON: Genuine?

JANE: The two experts who authenticated it came on the tour with us.

SOLOMON laughs.

JANE: *(Bridling.)* There's a very distinguished committee deciding what's genuine Rembrandt and what isn't. But it can't always be right, can it?

SOLOMON: Then what's the point of it?

JANE ignores this.

JANE: The special attraction was the de Brunne collection in Leyden. De Brunne has an example of every state of every etching Rembrandt ever made.

SOLOMON: Wow!

JANE: Unfortunately he thinks everyone wants to steal it. So it took me three years to persuade him to let us in. And that was only after Gargarov lent him one of his other yachts to go round the coast of Turkey.

WILLIAM: Were the etchings worth waiting for?

JANE: To tell you the truth, it was very stuffy in the chateau, and there was a moment I thought I was going to sneeze all over a unique print of Abraham sacrificing Isaac. I thought I'd be sacrificed too.

SOLOMON: Poor Jane!

She resents this.

JANE: It's humiliating, having to spend my time buttering up the filthy rich. Then – all this new stuff – Rembrandt and the Renaissance I can do. The Impressionists. The Post-Impressionists. But these installations everywhere – they're quite beyond me. I had to take some people to see the

Turner Prize last month. One of them actually *liked* it. I
didn't know what to say.

WILLIAM: We can always get someone younger to do the
contemporary.

JANE: Bernard thinks it's time I stopped.

WILLIAM: You don't want to move into management? Be
Chief Executive, for instance?

JANE: No. I don't believe in women being on top.

*KATE hears this, manages a smile at SOLOMON, then turns her
back quickly.*

JANE: I mean, you read all these things about women saying
they haven't been given a fair chance. Discrimination
and so on. But they're terribly pushy, aren't they? It's not
natural.

WILLIAM: Ah. 'Natural'!

JANE: Bernard thinks it would only make trouble to have a
woman as Chief Executive. As a matter of fact, he thinks
his connections in the financial world might be very useful
in –

WILLIAM: Oh, no, no. Not Bernard.

JANE: *(Angry.)* Why not?

WILLIAM: Because he – he doesn't inspire confidence. In me.

JANE: *(Exploding.)* Do you realize, you've never said a single
kind thing about Bernard since the day you met him! But
he's a wonderful father to the girls, a wonderful husband
to me, and we've lived a decent, proper life, not lied to
everyone about ourselves like you! I don't know how you
can live with yourself, living a lie like that all these years!
I'm just glad Mummy's not still alive to find out about it!

SOLOMON: Steady, Jane.

JANE: Now, I suppose, you'll want him to run the business!

SOLOMON: No thanks!

TOM appears. WILLIAM is very relieved to see him.

TOM: What's going on?

WILLIAM: I'm being abused. Probably rightly.

JANE: It's time you knew what we feel!

WILLIAM: Well, now I do. And thank you.

(To TOM.) What's the score?

JANE moves away, blowing her nose loudly.

TOM: Village all out for ninety-four.

WILLIAM: Not very good.

TOM: I don't know. It's only fifteen overs a side. And a very slow outfield.

SOLOMON: There were cows in there till last week. Seen Hugo?

TOM: He was talking to Evan Prichard.

SOLOMON: Getting on all right, were they?

TOM: Seemed to be.

WILLIAM: Of course they get on, they're both trouble-makers.

(Glad to talk business not family matters.) Tom, I've been thinking. Suppose the company decided to – not take you over, you wouldn't want that – but to support you through your temporary difficulties. We could, for instance, lend you the two million you want at half a per cent over bank rate, which is now so low as to be invisible. And we could allow you to pay the money back over a generous number of years.

TOM is silent.

WILLIAM: It would be better than letting it fall into the hands of the receivers, surely?

TOM: *(Beat.)* Actually I need three million. Three and a half.

WILLIAM: Why did you say only two?

TOM: I thought you'd call me an idiot.

WILLIAM: Well – But as far as the company's concerned, two million, three – what's the difference?

TOM: But if you're no longer running it –

WILLIAM: I could do you a safe enough deal before we sell. If we do.

(Eager to be liked.) You'd never get such terms from a new owner. You might not get any terms at all. There are advantages to a family-run business.

TOM: But it isn't family-run. It's run by you. Which is why I left.

WILLIAM: You thought I ran it badly?

TOM: You'd never let me make my own decisions. You checked every deal I made. You treated me like a child. A schoolboy. You never encouraged me, ever.

WILLIAM: *(To SOLOMON.)* I'm not doing very well this afternoon, am I?

(To TOM.) You never complained.

TOM: Have you any idea what complaining to you *about* you would be like?

Silence.

SOLOMON: Have you, William?

WILLIAM: *(Beat.)* No, I suppose not.

TOM: So I don't want the company to lend me money. Because I don't want to be under your thumb again. And if you sell it, I'll have more than enough from my share of Mum's half.

WILLIAM: But would she have wanted that?

TOM: Why should you be the only person to decide? She meant for us to have the money. Before we're dead.

JANE: *(Recovered.)* Yes, why can't we decide for ourselves? We're not children.

WILLIAM: *(Fighting back.)* But look what Tom's done. Got involved with a blatant crook, then come running to his dead Mummy to –

SOLOMON: William!

WILLIAM: Sorry.

(Cooler.) I think she'd say no.

TOM: You just don't want to let go. You want to keep the company, the money, everything in your own hands. You want to control us to your dying day.

WILLIAM feels very undermined. HUGO appears.

WILLIAM: Ah, Hugo. You'd better have your go.

HUGO: At what?

WILLIAM: Attacking me.

HUGO: Where shall I start?

WILLIAM: *(Unhappy laugh.)* What do you think?

HUGO: About what?

WILLIAM: Selling the company.

HUGO: You know what I think.

WILLIAM makes an effort.

WILLIAM: I've had an idea which might make you change your mind. Suppose we go in for Antiquarian Travel.

HUGO looks at SOLOMON, who just shrugs. The family listen to WILLIAM with stony faces.

WILLIAM: Today, all travel is horrible. Endless waits in overcrowded airports, interminable delays in railway stations as trains are cancelled, traffic jams on motorways – Ghastly. The solution is – go back to horse-drawn carriages!

HUGO: Dad –

WILLIAM: When did any of you last look at anything but the road ahead? But from a carriage you can see over hedges. See the country. Life at the speed of horses – six miles an hour – it could revolutionize the business.

TOM: Bankrupt it, more like.

WILLIAM: No, no, it will take our clients where they've always really wanted to go. The beautiful peaceful past. Paradise before the fall.

HUGO: You'd have to close all roads to motor traffic. Or your tourists would choke to death on exhaust fumes.

TOM: To say nothing of horseshit.

WILLIAM: *(To JANE.)* Susie would love it.

JANE: Susie may not be clever, but she has more sense than to go on main roads on a horse.

SOLOMON: Perhaps not the right moment, William.

WILLIAM: *(Deflated.)* Apparently not.

KATE has been drifting slowly back towards the others.

WILLIAM: What do you think? They all want me to sell, Kate.

KATE: I think you shouldn't.

TOM groans.

JANE: As we might have expected!

KATE: Just because you're giving up being Chief Executive doesn't mean we should give up the company. You should appoint one of us in your place. Me.

JANE: Please!

KATE: *(Very cool, to JANE.)* I just had a phone call. From Mr Dunwoody.

JANE: *(Aghast.)* Dunwoody? But you're not – you're not – Are you?

HUGO: Who's Dunwoody?

KATE: Our gynaecologist.

WILLIAM is astonished.

KATE: I thought, before I got married, I should have a check-up. I went last week. And I'm very glad I did. Because Mr Dunwoody's got the results of the tests and – and I'm carrying a faulty gene.

(To WILLIAM.) Got it from you, I dare say. Any child I have will almost certainly be brain-damaged.

Complete silence. WILLIAM is shattered.

KATE: I don't know how Milo will take it. But it simplifies things for me. I was going to take a break from work to have kids, but if I'm to be – childless – then – I want to run the company.

JANE: But you can't!

KATE: You want to retire to horses and saddle soap. Tom wants to dive in the South Pacific. Hugo is far too busy alerting us all to disaster to attend to business. So here I am.

WILLIAM: Kate, sweetheart –

KATE: *(Frown at him.)* Mum was running the business with you while she had us. She could be herself within the company. And so can I. But I can't be if you're still there, specially as chairman.

WILLIAM: Oh, but –

KATE: You'll interfere. Won't be able to help yourself. I must be free to make my own decisions. And I won't be if I have to keep kowtowing to you.

WILLIAM: But –

KATE: It's either that or we sell.

Silence. JANE raises her hand.

JANE: I'm even more for selling. And so is Bernard.

WILLIAM: Tom?

TOM: I don't know.

WILLIAM: *(Appealing.)* Kate –

KATE: The condition is irrevocable.

WILLIAM turns to SOLOMON.

WILLIAM: Solomon –

JANE: He's not family!

SOLOMON: *(Taking charge.)* I am, you know. And I think Kate will make an excellent Chief Executive.

JANE: She'll be – she'll be – Kate!

SOLOMON: Exactly. I also think it's a mistake to keep people in the company who don't want her to run it. So she should dismiss Jane.

JANE: Sack me! I'll resign first, thank you!

SOLOMON: You'd do better not to. Get compensation. You probably won't want it as a lump sum –

JANE: Yes I will!

SOLOMON: But your school fees will go on for several years. It'll be better to take the money as a sort of pension. Less tax.

WILLIAM: Wait a minute –

SOLOMON: The capital amount can be deducted from her
share of Valerie's trust.

WILLIAM: *(Aghast.)* Solomon –

JANE: *(Suspicious, to WILLIAM.)* You've been planning this
together, haven't you? You and him?

WILLIAM: Never heard a word of it till this moment. I'm – I'm
flabbergasted.

(To SOLOMON.) What are you doing, taking charge of my
family?

SOLOMON: Our family.

WILLIAM: I don't want those girls –

SOLOMON: They're not yours. They're hers.

WILLIAM is defeated.

KATE: What about Tom?

SOLOMON: Similar. Give him what he wants. Take the cash
out of the reserves. Against his share of Valerie's shares,
when and if they're sold.

WILLIAM: But he'll lose it all again! Like he did before!

SOLOMON: That's his problem. All right, Tom?

TOM: Well – I think so, yes.

KATE: The new CEO thinks that could be a very sensible
solution.

WILLIAM: Wait a minute, I said!

SOLOMON: They've waited too long, William. Time is bearing
them away. Like an ever rolling stream. Leaving us behind.
You and I, we're always thinking about the past, how we've
got to where we are. Africa. Stratford. But now we've come

to a great good place. You've spent your life selling it as an idea. Now we've got the reality. And we should stop.

WILLIAM: I don't want to stop!

SOLOMON just looks at him.

WILLIAM: It's death, stopping.

SOLOMON: It's death if you don't stop.

Silence.

SOLOMON: Have a pill.

As he offers him the pillbox, the phone goes indoors.

SOLOMON: Damn, where did I leave the phone?

He goes in. Evening is beginning to come on.

WILLIAM looks at SUSIE's pillbox. He's about to hurl it away, when he catches KATE's eye.

WILLIAM: Fucking hell.

She shrugs.

JANE: This is all – This is – I must speak to Bernard.

KATE turns to TOM.

KATE: What do you think, Tom?

TOM: I think I need to talk to Jack Warburton, but –

KATE: Go ahead.

TOM: Will you excuse me?

TOM goes off, taking out his mobile. SOLOMON appears in the doorway.

SOLOMON: Susie's found the saddle soap!

JANE: No! Where was it?

SOLOMON: In her pony's manger. Under the hay.

JANE: That just shows you! She hadn't looked properly.

KATE: I'm so glad. Now her little bottom can bounce happily up and down on burnished leather all the livelong afternoon.

She turns away to hide tears.

JANE: She's learned her lesson, that's one good thing. Excuse me.

She goes, taking out her phone like TOM.

KATE: *(Determinedly cheerful.)* I hope Bernard *is* still at the office. Not off with some bird. It's not called Canary Wharf for nothing, you know.

WILLIAM: Bernard? No. Surely? Do you think?

KATE: Never can tell.

WILLIAM: *(To SOLOMON.)* For God's sake, what have you done? Those poor little girls –

SOLOMON: They'll be better off taking lessons from a real schoolmistress than their mother.

WILLIAM: *(Beat.)* You're not allowed to say that.

SOLOMON: Yes, I am. I've been family for almost seven hours now. I can say anything I like. How was Mr Prichard, Hugo?

HUGO: Friendly. Knows a lot about climate change. In fact he's wondering whether to put in solar panels, but there's not that much sunshine round here and –

SOLOMON: What about the spring?

HUGO: He agrees with me that water shortages are likely to get worse. So when I suggested you should have a legal agreement – not against each other, but for both of you, against potential outsiders – he said he thought it was a very interesting idea.

SOLOMON: There you are, William. Problem on the way to solution.

WILLIAM: But the man's a racist!

HUGO: He's a little ashamed of that. He says, any time you want duck eggs, Solomon, just give him a ring.

SOLOMON: Thank you! We want to be friends with the neighbours. Specially as we get older. As a matter of fact, William – you know we were thinking of doing up the small barn? So there'd be someone to look after the place when we're in London, and – well, in case – you know?

WILLIAM: *(Suspicious.)* Yes?

SOLOMON: Hugo's looking for somewhere to set up his online network.

WILLIAM and KATE look at HUGO.

KATE: Are you? Seriously?

HUGO: Yes.

KATE: But I'm depending on you to help run the company. You may be a pain in the arse sometimes, but you're a damned good businessman.

HUGO: I'm sorry. I couldn't live with myself if I made any sort of compromise with the travel business now.

Silence.

WILLIAM: *(To SOLOMON.)* If he can only live with himself like that, do you honestly think he could live with us too?

SOLOMON: Are you sure, Hugo?

HUGO: Yes.

SOLOMON: You compromised with Mr Prichard.

HUGO: That was different.

Silence.

SOLOMON: Well – I hope intransigence is its own reward. I hope you do save the world.

HUGO: Thanks. And I hope you'll both be happy. Time one of us said it.

(Little shiver.) It's getting cold. I'll get my sweater.

He goes.

KATE: So do I get the job?

WILLIAM: *(Sigh.)* I think you do, yes.

KATE: *(Deflated.)* Whoopee.

SOLOMON: Are you all right?

KATE: No. It seems so incredibly unfair, of all the people in the world –

SOLOMON: The world isn't fair.

Silence.

KATE: We wanted four.

Silence.

KATE: How am I going to tell him?

WILLIAM: The way you told us. You were completely convincing. You almost convinced me.

KATE: But I won't be able to act with him. And I wouldn't want to even if I could. I love him.

SOLOMON: How will he take it?

KATE: Oh, he won't believe it at first. Then, when he sees it's true – I suppose he might like the idea of a crazily different kind of family, but – No, why should he? He's like his father. Our father. The eldest Fanshawe is always called Milo, you see. Has been since 1744. Having a son and heir, it's part of the family business.

WILLIAM: Then –

KATE: Exactly.

> *(False cheerfulness.)* But there's always more fish in the sea, isn't there? He'll go back to trawling. And me – I'll go back to busily seeking and continual change.

WILLIAM: Oh, Kate –

KATE: *(Can't keep it up.)* You know what you said about your lover who tried to kill himself? How you felt desolate?

WILLIAM: I was being selfish. I felt there was no chance of my ever finding happiness.

KATE: I feel that now.

WILLIAM: But I have found it.

SOLOMON: And worth the wait, I hope?

KATE: What do you think Mum would have said?

WILLIAM: Oh, I think – well, if she was still here –

KATE: About me, not you. She gave up a lot to live her own life, didn't she?

WILLIAM: She didn't see it as giving things up.

KATE: Then I must be like her. Accept my inheritance. Hope it's not in the genes to lose my marbles so early, that's all.

SOLOMON: You're very brave.

KATE: No, I'm not. I'm really just – stunned.

SOLOMON: Drink?

KATE: No thanks. I'll go and take another turn round the rose garden till I can look on the bright side.

WILLIAM: Darling –

KATE: I think, you see, that with a bit of creative skullduggery, we could take advantage of the depression to undercut some of our rivals. Drive them out of the marketplace. It will mean being pretty ruthless, but I feel like a bit of ruthlessnesss at the moment. When are we having the samphire?

SOLOMON: Half past seven.

KATE: I'll be there.

She goes.

SOLOMON: Well. Happy birthday.

WILLIAM: Poor Kate. But have I really been such an awful father?

SOLOMON: You've been yourself.

WILLIAM: I tried. I really tried.

SOLOMON: *(Consoling.)* People think, because – people like us – our genes die with us, we have no stake in the future. But it's not true. Not true at all.

(Beat.) I must start cooking.

WILLIAM: Can I come with you?

SOLOMON: So long as you don't pick at the starters.

WILLIAM: I love sitting with you in the kitchen. You stirring things about in saucepans while we talk about everything on the great globe itself. While it's still here. Might I be allowed, as it's my birthday, a glass of something white and sharpish, with just a hint of lemon in the bouquet?

SOLOMON: Possibly.

WILLIAM: Then let's go.

Instead of wheeling himself off, he tries again to stand. He succeeds a moment, then begins to sway.

SOLOMON: Here, what are you doing?

WILLIAM: Pray you, undo this button.

SOLOMON: William!

SOLOMON grabs hold of WILLIAM as he sways.

WILLIAM: One of my little tests. Not very funny. Must give them up. Along with so much else. But let's see if I can walk straight after all that's happened this afternoon.

He takes a step, falters.

WILLIAM: No. It'll have to be the chair.

SOLOMON helps him back in. WILLIAM grasps his hand.

WILLIAM: I feel very old, Solomon.

SOLOMON kisses his hand.

SOLOMON: Sixty-seven's not old. The world is all before us.

WILLIAM: You can't really believe that.

SOLOMON: No. But we're not dead yet. Come on.

He starts to push him off.

WILLIAM: Stop that! I can manage!

He twirls the chair around, and they go into a little dance together, WILLIAM manipulating the chair, SOLOMON jigging around him.

JANE, then TOM, then KATE, then HUGO, come silently on and watch as the lights go down.

Lights down.